Woman of Flowers

by Siôn Eirian

After Saunders Lewis

and

The Royal Bed

by Siôn Eirian

An English Language Adaptation of Siwan by Saunders Lewis

First published by Atebol in 2018

Adeiladau'r Fagwyr, Llanfihangel Genau'r Glyn, Aberystwyth, Ceredigion SY24 5AQ

Text copyright © Siôn Eirian 2018

Design by Owain Hammonds

Cover design by Holly McCarthy

Printed and bound in Wales by Gwasg Gomer, Llandysul

ISBN: 978-1-912261-45-1

www.atebol.com

FOREWORD

Woman of Flowers and *The Royal Bed* are two short but epic dramas by the celebrated Welsh contemporary playwright Siôn Eirian. Both are inspired by the work of Saunders Lewis, widely hailed as the greatest Welsh language playwright.

Woman of Flowers is a new work based on the ancient Mabinogi myth of Blodeuwedd in which Siôn Eirian has skilfully combined original material with some of the iconic passages from Saunders Lewis's 1948 theatrical masterpiece *Blodeuwedd*. *The Royal Bed* is a translation and adaptation of Saunders's Lewis's other great verse-drama, *Siwan*, first performed in 1954.

At the centre of each play are women who transgress a moral code. Blodeuwedd, a woman created from flowers to be the perfect wife for the warrior prince Llew, asserts her innate wildness in the face of those who would control her. Siwan, the illegitimate daughter of King John and outspoken and politically astute wife of Llywelyn Prince of Gwynedd, puts passion before duty. For both women the repercussions for rebelling against a repressive social order established and patrolled by men are bloody and far-reaching.

Siôn Eirian (b.1954) is an award-winning Welsh dramatist who writes in Welsh and English. He is also a poet and in 1978, aged 24, won the bardic crown at the National Eisteddfod of Wales. This, together with his appointment in the same year as Theatr Clwyd's first resident playwright, marked the beginning of his professional writing career which has to date spanned forty years and encompassed stage, television and radio and included many ground-breaking and award-winning plays and adaptations.

Saunders Lewis (b.1893, d.1985) was born in in Wallasey, Wirral to a Welsh speaking family. He co-founded the Welsh Nationalist party Plaid Cymru in 1925 before establishing himself as a scholar and writer who dominated the academic and literary scene in Wales for decades. His literary output was varied and prodigious and he excelled in the genre of drama, in particular the difficult craft of verse drama. *Blodeuwedd* and *Siwan* are held by many to be the greatest plays ever written in the Welsh language.

Woman of Flowers and *The Royal Bed* were first produced by Theatr Pena, a Cardiff based, national touring theatre company renowned for its innovative staging of classic plays with memorable and strong female characters. **www.theatrpena.co.uk**

Woman of Flowers

by Siôn Eirian

After Saunders Lewis

Theatr Pena / Taliesin Arts Centre Co-Production

Woman of Flowers was first performed at Taliesin Arts Centre, Swansea on 1st February 2018 with the following cast:

ARIANRHOD	Betsan Llwyd
BLODEUWEDD	Sara Gregory
GWYDION	Eiry Thomas
LLEW	Oliver Morgan-Thomas
RHAGNELL	Olwen Rees
GRONW	Rhys Meredith

Director	Erica Eirian
Composer	Peter Knight
Movement Director	Caroline Lamb
Designer	Holly McCarthy
Lighting Designer	Kay Haynes
Cameraman	Peter Firth
Video Editor	Dafydd Hunt
Creative Producer	Ceri James

Production Manager	Richard Balshaw
Stage Manager	Brenda Knight
Technician and Relighter	Jon Cox
Set Construction	Telgwen
Scenic Artist	James Horne
Costume Supervisor	Deryn Tudor

Marketing Officer	Megan Merrett
Audio Describer, Swansea	Alastair Sill, Word of Mouth
Captioner and Operator, Cardiff	Erika James
Caption Operator, Mold	Stevie Burrows

Theatr Pena is grateful to the Welsh Assembly Government and the Arts Council of Wales, Curo Advisers Limited and their strategic partners and the following Theatr Pena 2017–18 Supporters for supporting this production:

Tom and Felicity Crawley
Sir Alan Cox, CBE
Julie and Bryn Davies
Barbara Francis
Jack and Susannah Hanbury-Tenison
Hugh Hudson-Davies, CVO
Julian Mitchell
Walter New
Fiona Peel, OBE
Michael and Ann Robinson
Stephen Shaw
Dr Tamsin Spargo
Stephen and Mary Walsh
Margaret Weakley
John and Judi Wilkins
William Wilkins, CBE, and Lynne Wilkins

WOMAN OF FLOWERS

CHARACTERS

ARIANRHOD

BLODEUWEDD

GWYDION

LLEW

RHAGNELL

GRONW

PROLOGUE

CAER ARIANRHOD, ARFON
A storm rages.

Enter ARIANRHOD.

In her mind's eye, Arianrhod sees BLODEUWEDD dancing with abandonment in the sleeting rain as howling winds splinter the boughs of the vast, ancient trees.

ARIANRHOD   Once again there's a war to be fought.
                    And the battleground will be that young body.
                    The little map of her flesh
                    Pure, perfect even,
                    Will be charred and scarred.
                    The men will do this of course.
                    As they always do. To her. To me.
                    Some of us survive. And are stronger for it.
                    As yet I've no idea whose side
                    This one wishes to take. Mine, or that bastard beast,
                    My sibling who makes the earth tremble and skies crash
                    And turns all living things into toys
                    To be played with, broken and discarded.

Arianrhod's thoughts turn to GWYDION.

ARIANRHOD   My sibling Gwydion who creates life but serves death.

GWYDION   Two weeks ago in Coetir woods
                  I was knocked to the ground by a wild boar
                  Twice my size. It mated with me.

ARIANRHOD   At the foot of my bed is an oak-wood chest.
                    It's empty. And always will be.
                    On it is a woven shawl
                    And some pelts of warm fur.
                    Here burrowed into the folds
                    Two small eyes squinting out
                    Is a fox cub. I found it, a stray
                    In the stable, hiding from the hounds.

GWYDION	Blood in my mouth, between my legs I dragged myself into a bracken lair And lay whimpering for five days and nights I was within a few miles of your fort But I knew you'd turn me away.
ARIANRHOD	Heal yourself wizard. What could I offer you?
GWYDION	I'm your sister your brother both. But You have more love for that fox cub.
ARIANRHOD	I feel for anything that's alone in the world. Cast aside. The weak, the defenceless They're the only ones I trust. And you're right. I wouldn't nurse you. Families bring grief. Their ties have left me A prisoner to solitude. I live alone.
GWYDION	Can't you hear me in the night Swirling through the hunchbacked trees.
ARIANRHOD	My fox warms me back to sleep And I dream of walking in sunlight In soft fine slippers in quiet courtyards Alone, always alone, in a white world.
GWYDION	I'm a bridge between her soft slippered feet And these beasts' trampling hooves. Now I'm angry. In my dreams I make flames shoot from black earth, I breathe out billowing banks of mist Which come to nudge and tug At the edges of Arianrhod's lands. I'm still your sister, your brother, your family You'll not be rid of me by wishing.
ARIANRHOD	Why are you here now? In my thoughts? Shouldn't you be with Llew in Ardudwy? He wants you. You're still family to him. Go to him. He pines for you. (*Exit Arianrhod.*)

ACT ONE

SCENE ONE

THE GREAT HALL, MUR Y CASTELL, ARDUDWY
In the far distance, the storm continues.

Enter LLEW.

Gwydion watches, unseen.

LLEW   Rhagnell. Rhagnell!

RHAGNELL   I'm coming.

LLEW   Rhagnell!

Enter RHAGNELL.

RHAGNELL   My Lord?

LLEW   Where's Blodeuwedd? In her chamber?

RHAGNELL   Her chamber? Ha! Never by choice.
                   I saw her walk towards the river in the woods.

LLEW   Go to her, and tell her this: my gifts for Math are ready.
                   We'll set out now while three hours of daylight still remain.
                   Gwydion and all the soldiers shall accompany me.

RHAGNELL   And she's to remain here?

LLEW   Yes. She'd better hurry if she wants to say goodbye.

RHAGNELL   I'll tell her. (*Exit Rhagnell.*)

ARIANRHOD   And you made him complete?
(*Voice from off*)

GWYDION   I gave him everything he lacked. Why?

ARIANRHOD   Why?
(*Voice from off*)   You won't find a man more wretched
                   In the whole of Gwynedd. Still inconsolable.

GWYDION	Not so. I've given him happiness.
ARIANRHOD (*Voice from off*)	He's a man now. But still miserable. He'll grow old before he's known happiness. You've given him keys to doors But the world he wants refuses to open for him. Time's running out.
GWYDION	Always so forlorn. I'm tired of your self-pity.
LLEW	Gwydion. Where have you been? We're ready.
GWYDION	I saved you. Protected you. Gave you a future. You had three callous fates placed upon you Yet I undid each one.
LLEW	No one could have wished for a better friend than you Gwydion.
GWYDION	No. Yet no one's been more badly rewarded for friendship Than me. There was my brother Gilfaethwy. I had to live Among the wild animals for years because of him, Not knowing my place in the world, one day male, The next female, creating a freakish family. And now you. Who knows what misfortunes You'll bring upon me. You whose own mother Would have destroyed you had I not intervened.
LLEW	A mother's loathing outweighs an uncle's love.
GWYDION	How is that? Every ruse of hers was thwarted. When she Denied you a name, I construed your naming. She decreed that you shall not carry weapons, I tricked her into arming you with her own hands. She destined that you may never find a wife born of man: I spun for you from wild flowers a maiden Better than any eye has seen.
LLEW	But I still haven't escaped my mother's vengeance. Blodeuwedd isn't like other women.
GWYDION	Indeed. In all my great span of spell making

	I've loved many a girl and beast – and never yet Did I find one woman to be like another.
LLEW	She won't bear my children. Isn't that so Gwydion?
GWYDION	I can't remember Arianrhod's precise words.
LLEW	I can. "He won't have a wife of woman born, And won't have children of his own". Those words are chiselled in my memory. Is it a fate you can't circumvent? Will you fail?
GWYDION	A child can be a mixed blessing. The last one I had....was a wolf. In every other way Llew, Blodeuwedd is perfection.
LLEW	I'll never forget that shimmering morning When I first saw her, naked as that dawn itself, The dew still glistening on her white breasts, Breasts as pure as a snowdrop's petals When the night furls their swell. She walked, The soul of that virgin spring in a flawless mould of flesh. I looked at her, and she at me. I clothed her nakedness with kisses And these arms, these awkward arms, Which had been empty so long, encircled her. But she was cold, so cold. I've never seen A trace of a blush upon her cheeks, only a pallid glow, Like that of the moon casting its random light On the world below. Her very blood is alien. She won't ever belong. To anyone. She's closer to the wild animals in the forest Than she is to me. That's her world. You know that.
GWYDION	And I know both worlds. In these arms I've held a range Of females, and believe me lad, on a warm spring morning It's the same feel to the softest girl's skin and a hog's hide.
LLEW	One foul night of howling gales and sleeting rain, She ran from my bed and into the storm's rage. I followed – full of suspicion and anger

Beneath my cloak a sword. But no one came to her.
Not even the wolves were out on such a night.
Yet there she was, dancing to the tempest's fury.

GWYDION   You can't cleave a creature from its kindred.

LLEW   I was frightened and called out. But she didn't hear.
And with the wind lashing trees and splintering boughs
I was lost in a fearful world
Where the only things that held their own
Were rock and rain, the stormy dark,
And her, Blodeuwedd....I ran after her,
Shouted louder, grasped her arm ...
"You've caught me" she said, suddenly sad
Like a child woken from some distant dream
"You've caught me. Let's go home."
And I saw, in that night's storm
That I had no place in her life.
Why does a heart of ice lie beneath a breast
That excites desire like the first sun of summer.

Enter Blodeuwedd.

BLODEUWEDD   I received your message.

LLEW   Yes lady, we must go.

BLODEUWEDD   And Gwydion too?

LLEW   Gwydion too.

BLODEUWEDD   The day's short, and soon it'll be night.
Llew, stay here. I don't want
To spend tonight without you.

LLEW   You won't be alone.
You have your maid, and many servants.

BLODEUWEDD   I've never parted from you before;
It frightens me, being left here.

LLEW   Since when?

BLODEUWEDD	My spirit's restless. Wait for tomorrow's dawn; The sun will speed your journey to Caer Dathl.
LLEW	No. Everyone's ready. We must go, Math the king expects us.
BLODEUWEDD	Magician – am I beautiful? Are you pleased with your work?
GWYDION	I'll tell you this my girl. Your beauty's unmatched. You're the masterpiece of all my magic.
BLODEUWEDD	But you did me a disfavour when you chained My free nature with flesh and sinew And placed me in this world Where favours must be asked of husbands And then not granted. And these codes That I can't comprehend. I should despise you And yet my instinct is to like you. You too spent summers beneath the leaves. You know the feel of earth on flesh And the sounds of nature's stirrings in the grass.
GWYDION	Ssh. Don't talk about that here – it shames me.
BLODEUWEDD	I don't know what it is to be ashamed ... Stay with me until my lord returns. Protect me.
LLEW	Come uncle, it's time to leave.
GWYDION	Farewell my little petal girl. I'm old as oak. You'd soon tire of my company. The heady smells of spring surround you still, The blooms I beaded to form your features Haven't withered. Stay young, forever. Farewell.
BLODEUWEDD	Shall we three ever be together again? My heart's heavy. Farewell.

(*Exit Gwydion.*)

Llew, if you believed me you wouldn't go today.

LLEW	My life can't be ruled on a girl's whim.
BLODEUWEDD	I know the seasons better than you. I sense each change in wind and rain and sun. Why shouldn't I also read the seasons of a man?
LLEW	Don't be afraid. I'm destined That no harm will easily befall me. And you be wise. Don't stray too far from home. Don't let the woodlands tempt you out at dusk, But stay among my people here, Be your best Blodeuwedd. I'll only be three days. Farewell, farewell. (*Exit Llew.*)

Enter Rhagnell.

BLODEUWEDD	He didn't listen. He doesn't see.
RHAGNELL	Three days, no more.
BLODEUWEDD	That's all it took to make me. How much less To unmake me. For me to become nothing again. Llew too fears the future. And he fears me.
RHAGNELL	What makes you say that, child?
BLODEUWEDD	Before you came to seek me, in the woods, I could hear them talking.
RHAGNELL	Him and Gwydion. From the woods?
BLODEUWEDD	I have a kestrel's eye, a bat's ear.
RHAGNELL	Don't tell me that you can fly as well.
BLODEUWEDD	In my dreams I do.
RHAGNELL	We all do that. Even me. Who's too old to run Or to even see my path as I used to.
BLODEUWEDD	Why did they give me you as a maid?
RHAGNELL	What I lack in steadiness I make up for with wisdom. Gwydion knows that. I have the knowledge that you lack.

BLODEUWEDD	Llew hates his mother. I know that.
RHAGNELL	No. But she resents him. And he despairs.
BLODEUWEDD	You know her history. Perhaps that's why Gwydion chose you. You're meant to tell me.
RHAGNELL	Her history is that shame begets shame.
BLODEUWEDD	How? I need you to tell me. There's a history behind my being. But I feel I've no past and no future. Who am I Rhagnell?
RHAGNELL	You're woman Blodeuwedd. That gives you enough past And future to carry with you.

(*She pauses.*)

I'll tell you about Arianrhod's shame.
It will make you marvel at the world you've entered.
Arianrhod and Gwydion grew up in the court
Of their uncle, the Great King Math.
So did their brother Gilfaethwy, an evil one, by all accounts.
King Math had a foot maid. A young innocent.
Gilfaethwy raped her. The brute. And apparently
With Gwydion's help. Though I find that hard to believe.
As punishment the brothers were banished to the woods,
And turned into animals. I've heard it said
They were forced to mate with each other
And became father and mother to various beasts.
After three years, their penance done, they returned to Math's
   court.

BLODEUWEDD	And Arianrhod?
RHAGNELL	Gwydion proposed her as Math's new foot maid. He accepted. But first, to prove her virginity Before the assembled court she had to step over a magic wand. Imagine her shock when during the test

She gave birth to a sturdy boy.
Math named him Dylan and he ran from the fortress
Till he found the sea and swam away.
In shame Arianrhod ran from the court but as she ran
Something small dropped from her womb.
Arianrhod didn't pause to look at it.
Gwydion picked the thing up and secreted it in a chest
In his chamber where it survived and grew.

BLODEUWEDD   And became Llew?

RHAGNELL   He did. Gwydion adopted him.
In her anger Arianrhod cursed the boy and decreed
He wouldn't have a name or weapons or a wife.

BLODEUWEDD   My part in this.

RHAGNELL   Yes, Gwydion has spent his life
Righting the wrongs Llew suffered.
Gilfaethwy died. No one mourned him.
Arianrhod lives alone, outside society.

BLODEUWEDD   Poor Arianrhod. And that little foot maid.
The women fared badly in this history.

RHAGNELL   Now Blodeuwedd, has that helped
You forget your own small despair?

BLODEUWEDD   No Rhagnell. It's reminded me
That I was made solely for his happiness.
But now, I'll have time to dwell on my own thoughts.
My lord has gone away!

RHAGNELL   Why should you be afraid? This is your fortress.
These are your lands and here your word is law.
There's no one here who doesn't love you.
I would lay down my life for you if need be.

BLODEUWEDD   No. It's not men I fear
But being on my own – this solitude.
My lord has gone away!

RHAGNELL   What is this?
           I've heard you countless times wanting to flee
           And heard you curse the man who made you wife.
           Why this change?

BLODEUWEDD   You'll never understand my agony.
             You don't know the loneliness that gnaws.
             Your world's full – you've got a home.
             Loved ones, family, sisters, brothers,
             You're not an alien in this world.
             Wherever mankind walks, you have familiar paths
             And all of Gwynedd, where your forebears lived,
             Is your hearth. That's something I don't have.
             There's no headstone with a family name for me
             In this world I'm rootless, set apart.
             That's why I fear. What's that noise?

RHAGNELL   Someone far off hunting in the woods.

BLODEUWEDD   My lord's gone away. Between us
             There was never any passion. He knows nothing
             Of the dark desires woven into my nature
             And I know nothing of his nobility.
             His tame mind, his joy in friendships
             Yet without him and Gwydion
             I'm totally adrift and unanchored
             With nature's wild waves surging in my blood.
             God be my witness – I don't want the blame
             When this harm falls upon us.

RHAGNELL   That hunt's getting closer. You can see them now.

BLODEUWEDD   Yes. They're in full cry. Look!
             The stag's hooves are skimming the earth
             Like oars hitting spume. The scenting dogs
             Bound over the trail, and thundering horses
             Pound out the passing furlongs. Nature
             At its glorious best, full of breathless beauty.
             The hunter as one with the vibrant land –
             I could love a hunter –

RHAGNELL	Why d'you think they've stopped?
BLODEUWEDD	The horses are exhausted, the stag's escaped. They know that it'll soon be dark. Where are they from d'you think?
RHAGNELL	Shouldn't we offer them shelter for the night? They're looking at our fort. Turning their horses Towards us. Blodeuwedd?
BLODEUWEDD	Yes, offer them shelter. Food. Wine. I can't let my lord find fault with me For turning a nobleman away As dusk unseats the day.
RHAGNELL	Lady, this is how you should be, Full of warmth and welcome. I'll go And talk to their lord. You, stay light of heart Set sorrows aside. (*Exit Rhagnell.*)
BLODEUWEDD	My beating breast, has the hour come? Freedom, excitement; these are my real masters And my imperative is lust – the lust that drives the seed To prise through a shroud of earth to reach the sun. There's a shoot in me that seeks the light And wants to flourish and burst into fruit Without a blade to prune it back. I know That this huntsman is an emperor of passion; I know the music of a horn – it wasn't my husband's Thin lips that pursed to blow those lusty calls But stronger lips, swelling with blood red bloom, A much more fitting match for mine.

Rhagnell returns.

RHAGNELL	Lady, Gronw Pebr, Lord of Penllyn Is the man. He waits to greet you.
BLODEUWEDD	How barren are those words. A brazen bugle Not a wench's tongue should announce that name. Let's go to welcome him. (*Exeunt.*)

INTERLUDE

CAER ARIANRHOD, ARFON

Enter Arianrhod.

ARIANRHOD   Women take in strays and strangers.
Offering solace, seeking love.
I'm drawn to the wounded and the wanting.
Perhaps to atone for failing my runt of a son.
Gwydion found some softness in her heart
And reared it. That was atonement too.
It gave Gwydion purpose. But it gave me my weakness.
I'm easily tricked.
Gwydion and Llew came to my fort disguised and
Stole from me weapons and a name
And undid my curses.
For Blodeuwedd now the danger
Is not what might be taken from her, but what she finds.
She'll feast on new fruit and hunger for more. (*Exit Arianrhod.*)

ACT ONE
SCENE TWO

THE WOODS, MUR Y CASTELL, ARDUDWY

Enter Gronw and Blodeuwedd.

BLODEUWEDD   Have you had enough?

GRONW   Of food and drink, yes.

BLODEUWEDD   What else is there?

GRONW   Don't ask.

BLODEUWEDD   Are you afraid of saying?

GRONW   I don't fear anything
Except for losing honour.

BLODEUWEDD   Fear never caught a stag, or woman.

GRONW   Is there a way from here back to Penllyn
Through the dark? I've not hunted this far before.

BLODEUWEDD   Yes. Over the hills where loping wolves
Howl their hunger at the high moon.

GRONW   Is there a servant who could show us the way?

BLODEUWEDD   No one would dare do that. Except me.

GRONW   You?

BLODEUWEDD   The night and I are cousins
And wolves don't hunt the scent of flowers.

GRONW   I've heard things. We all have.
Is it true you were conjured from wild flowers?

BLODEUWEDD   Do you see these?

(She scoops a handful of leaves and petals from the woodland floor.)

You could imagine

Their beauty is eternal, and yet they're dead.
Dropped wings of vibrant colour
Now pale and faded, fallen to the floor.

(*She pauses.*)

Would you say I'm beautiful?

GRONW   The world's rose.

BLODEUWEDD   But I'm fading too. I've got no root among men.
A wizard plundered nature's bloom, cut it
And put it on display in a stone hall.
I was wrenched by that uncaring hand
And put here to serve my purpose and to die.

GRONW   What do you want?

BLODEUWEDD   Tell me your secret
Then I'll tell you what I want.

GRONW   From the moment I saw you, I wanted you.

BLODEUWEDD   And is that why you want to leave me tonight?

GRONW   You're already married – Am I not
Duty bound to respect his rights?

BLODEUWEDD   Duty? Rights? What are they Gronw?

GRONW   Oh, I'm so lost in my lust for you,
That I can't think of duty or honour now.
This face, my fair creature, this body
Fills me with wild excitement.

BLODEUWEDD   So no more talk of leaving?

GRONW   No.

BLODEUWEDD   Choose between me and your peers and your honour.
Their sober morals, honed by civilisation;
And my unfettered kisses and my lust.
And think before you choose. From them

The security of lifelong friends, a future partner
Perhaps, to share your estate and life,
Traditions and expectations to smother you,
An honourable burial in your forebears' vault
And dutiful children to carry your coffin.
With me there's no security beyond the present
He who loves me must love danger, and tread
The lonely road to freedom. In his life
He'll have no friends, no family to nurse him
To his grave. Only this wild cascade of hair
To swamp his senses, and these, my breasts
To give him blissful moments
And here, now shall be his heaven ... You choose.

GRONW I've chosen.

BLODEUWEDD Come lover,
We lay claim to life – and to make love is to be free.

They are overwhelmed by desire for each other.

Blodeuwedd draws Gronw deeper into the woods. (Exeunt.)

INTERLUDE

CAER ARIANRHOD, ARFON

Enter Arianrhod.

ARIANRHOD   Three days ago I woke and the cub was gone.
                       His scent stays on this blanket. I'll put
                       A fresh pelt in its place. Last year
                       A fledgling kestrel was blown down
                       From a nest high in the battlements.
                       That one stayed with me for two weeks.
                       I fed it scraps of meat and watched
                       Its yellow pebble eyes get to know me,
                       Its hooked beak, soft rimmed, seek out my hand.
                       I wish that Math had taken me as his pupil
                       And tutored me in the making of live things.
                       Gwydion gathered the most perfect petals
                       And most delicate fronds from broom and meadowsweet
                       And young oak leaves burnished by spring sun
                       Rubbed supple by saliva and sweat and tears
                       Gathered from young girls in feverish nights
                       And wove and beaded and teased these into life.
                       To make her. But nothing in that preparation
                       Endowed her with rationality or responsibility
                       No sense of duty, no honour.
                       How could perfection have neglected
                       The crowning achievements of the human mind?
                       If I'd had his skills I would have fashioned
                       A small soft animal or bird, weak and timid
                       Whose loyalty was to the giver of food and warmth.
                       The sense of duty bred by grateful dependence.
                       Yes, I'd have made a companion, a comfort
                       To spare my nights from being endless things. (*Exit Arianrhod.*)

ACT TWO

SCENE ONE

BLODEUWEDD'S CHAMBER, MUR Y CASTELL, ARDUDWY

Enter Blodeuwedd and Gronw.

GRONW
My captain says the horses are ready
My men want to leave.

BLODEUWEDD
Must you go?

GRONW
Or stay here and be killed.

BLODEUWEDD
No my love. If there's to be a kill
It won't be you.

GRONW
He and his men return today.

BLODEUWEDD
Yes. Go then. Don't delay. His name tolls
Like a death knell in this heart.
Do you know, in the woodlands in June
When the golden seed adorns the blackbird's beak
And the leaves' murmuring is louder than the sound of the
stream ...
Then, suddenly, all becomes still.
The sweet piping stops, the hedgerows silent.
And in the roots and stems the sap's rise is arrested ...
And in that moment the leaves grow old
As the summer bears down
On the bushes. And spring dies. So too for me
That, in the first steps of love's dance,
I'm suddenly reminded of him.
His name, his being, and I stumble to a halt.

GRONW
Blodeuwedd, Is this our lot?

BLODEUWEDD
I tasted joy. I never had this before.
Now I'm happy. I know who I am.

GRONW
Three nights of blissful sin.
Is that our destiny then?

BLODEUWEDD   It's fulfilment. For now.
              It's what I craved. It made me happy.

GRONW   I daren't stay. But I want more of you.

BLODEUWEDD   Our bodies are inexhaustible. O, Gronw,
              I want to delve into all their riches with you.
              To wake up all our senses with our coupling.
              And then too the seasons of our stillness,
              The peace of sleep, beside you,
              In your arms, knowing as I wake
              That we'll make love again, and again.
              How can I go back to sleeping with him?
              Lying there unfulfilled. Not wanting him,
              His awkward approaches, his timid touching.
              Then me watching him sleeping,
              Alongside me. A stranger.

GRONW   You don't want
              This day to mark the end of our love?

BLODEUWEDD   No. No!

GRONW   And Llew Llaw Gyffes?

BLODEUWEDD   Why do you say his name?

GRONW   We must look upon our fear
              And name it.

BLODEUWEDD   Is there some trick, to deceive Llew?

GRONW   Yes. Come away with me. This morning, now.

BLODEUWEDD   Where?

GRONW   To my fortress.
              The horses stand ready at the gates.
              Our freedom is in those stirrups. Let the Llew
              Come to his lair and find it empty.
              From my battlements we'll brave his roar.

BLODEUWEDD	You don't know his strength. Behind him stands Math
	And the massive might of Gwynedd
	And Gwydion the sorcerer. No fort on earth
	Can repel them. And I don't want
	To be caught like some doe in this lion's claws,
	My flesh ripped to shreds.
GRONW	Blodeuwedd, what's a court
	Or a kingdom to us? We'll flee to far Dyfed
	Where Math's enemies will welcome us
	And give us sanctuary.
BLODEUWEDD	I'll never go. I can't impose myself on strangers.
	It's easy for you to trust their word. Not me.
GRONW	Man is more caring than you credit.
BLODEUWEDD	To his kind. But as I'm outside their pack,
	Why should they offer their trust?
	Don't take me away from here.
GRONW	What shall we do?
BLODEUWEDD	Kiss. Forget. And farewell.
GRONW	Is that your advice?
BLODEUWEDD	I don't know any better.
GRONW	Can you forget all this?
BLODEUWEDD	No. Never.
GRONW	D' you want to forget?
BLODEUWEDD	Do you?
GRONW	I'd rather die.
BLODEUWEDD	Kiss me, my lover ... Before long
	He'll claim again the homage of these lips
	His hands will grasp at these shoulders
	And mark out his demands on this white flesh.

I wish there was a poison in my teeth,
So that like a serpent I could coil around his neck,
Constricting him, and crush him in an embrace
Like this ... like this ...
My fangs would finish him.

GRONW   Enough Blodeuwedd.
               But that's the only way. We must kill him.

BLODEUWEDD   It's taken you this long to read my mind.

GRONW   I wouldn't wish him dead, unless it has to happen

BLODEUWEDD   It has to. You know it has to.

GRONW   Is there a way to kill him?

BLODEUWEDD   It won't be easy. He's fated
               That he can only die in a certain way.
               But he's the sole possessor of that secret.

GRONW   So fate is set against our love?

BLODEUWEDD   Love's a rare bloom. It grows
               Up on the cliff of death. Some snatch at it.
               Others graze upon it gently. Patience Gronw.

GRONW   How do we discover the secret of his death?

BLODEUWEDD   Leave that to me. These slender fingers
               Can play his hungry body like a harp,
               Can lull him, lure from him
               The secret sealed inside his heart.
               He'll return today, lonely and restive
               And I shall kiss him.

GRONW   And prise from him the greatest mystery he possesses.

BLODEUWEDD   A soul for a kiss. Is the price too much?

GRONW   These moments with you, or my previous life.
               If I had to choose between the two
               Like a moth to a flame I'd fly to you.

BLODEUWEDD   Yes. I know. What's our plan?

GRONW   Leave that to me. If a man's hand
             Can destroy him – send me word.
             And when our day comes to hatch this plot
             I'll count each hour I've been away from you
             And in the blow that splices him
             I'll count each morning, noon and night
             Of missing you.... I must go.

BLODEUWEDD   You'll keep your word?

GRONW   Do you doubt my fidelity?

BLODEUWEDD   Gronw – what does your fidelity mean to me?
             Will you still want me? Desire is what holds
             Man's will a slave and keeps its arrow true
             When fidelity's bow has rusted. Look at me,
             Feast your lips upon this kiss
             And fill your nostrils with my scent ... Now go.

GRONW   Shall I hear from you tonight?

BLODEUWEDD   Before nightfall. (*Exeunt.*)

INTERLUDE

CAER ARIANRHOD, ARFON

Dusk, the same day.

Enter Arianrhod.

ARIANRHOD   Deep in my mind I see them ride
Gronw's rippling muscles, horses' mouths foam-flecked
As hooves hit sparks from rock, and then...
The horses' wheel, and rear. A dead stag
They'd killed in their earlier hunting
But hadn't returned to butcher, lies on the path.
We know why. Gronw had found a sweeter meat
To feast on. Now this forgotten carcass
Has been blown big by three days hot sun
Then punctured and opened by tearing beaks.
Two ravens slowly strut, waiting their turn
While a huge white headed eagle straddles ribs,
Tearing at entrails, dipping into puddles of dark blood,
Its white feathers soaked red. The stench of death
Hangs from the air. A noble beast left out to rot.
That's not the proper huntsman's practised way.
But over cold custom now feverish needs holds sway.
    (*Exit Arianrhod.*)

ACT TWO
SCENE TWO

THE GREAT HALL, MUR Y CASTELL, ARDUDWY

Enter Blodeuwedd and Rhagnell.

RHAGNELL   I was looking to the North. I saw
Dust clouds on the horizon. Llew's approaching.

BLODEUWEDD   What shall we do?

RHAGNELL   Three days and nights you and Penllyn's lord
Have lain here. Now we must hide
All these traces of your loving.

BLODEUWEDD   Could you kill for love sweet Rhagnell?

RHAGNELL   Killing and loving are opposites.

BLODEUWEDD   Not always.

RHAGNELL   In so many ways you're still a child
And what does a child know?

BLODEUWEDD   Its own mind.

RHAGNELL   I'll prepare food and drink.

BLODEUWEDD   For whom?

RHAGNELL   For you and your lord, your husband.

BLODEUWEDD   And serve them to us in a grave.

RHAGNELL   Come, Lady, make ready to receive him.
I'll go and greet him.

BLODEUWEDD   Yes, go. Tell him my secret too.

RHAGNELL   Do you think I'd betray you?

BLODEUWEDD   You're born of a woman's womb, like him.

RHAGNELL	And I'm also your maid for as long as I draw breath.
BLODEUWEDD	No, no. You shan't mock me. I know My looks can turn a young man's head And make him wild, a slave to my will. But you're a woman and I can never chain you.
RHAGNELL	A different chain ties me.

Blodeuwedd looks at Rhagnell and takes the ribbons which adorn her dress and draws them into circles around the maid's throat and nape.

BLODEUWEDD	Yes, you have your chains. These ribbons Soft as silk. Why don't you Wear them like a torque around your throat, A present from your mistress, A reward for your loyalty. Wear them tight, Tight enough to choke you Rhagnell. Wise and mute, forever the guardian of my secret.
RHAGNELL	You're hurting me. Do you want to kill me?
BLODEUWEDD	I want to tie up this fragile neck with this silk, So that not one traitorous utterance Shall pass through these pale lips That used to kiss my hand each night ... You've waited on me countless times, Sweet Rhagnell. You've soothed me to sleep. Now I can tend to you, and rock you To a deeper sleep than I've experienced ever.
RHAGNELL	Alive or dead, I won't betray you.
BLODEUWEDD	You won't get that chance, old woman; I'll lock your tongue inside these lips In case you're ever tempted.
RHAGNELL	He's here.

Enter Llew.

LLEW	I've arrived sooner than expected? I sped on ahead of my soldiers To see Blodeuwedd first.
BLODEUWEDD	Here I am.
LLEW	My fair, my flawless wife.
BLODEUWEDD	You journeyed safely?
LLEW	Today the wonder of your beauty is the same As on that first morning, when the dew Glistened in your footsteps. Fair wife I didn't know the power of your spell Until I felt its loss.
BLODEUWEDD	You've never been away from me before.
LLEW	Nor will I again until I die.
BLODEUWEDD	Let that be true.
LLEW	What did you do while I was away?
BLODEUWEDD	Ask Rhagnell. Tell him woman. Here's your chance.
RHAGNELL	Master, since Blodeuwedd first came to Ardudwy I've been at her side, day and night. I never saw a tear stain her cheek Nor well up in her eye. She kept her own counsel And reined in emotion. But the day You left here, I found her Lying here, wailing and weeping, Her body racked by loss and worry. The only answer I could prise from her To all my questions was "My Lord has left". (*Exit Rhagnell.*)
LLEW	Oh, wife, why wasn't I Allowed to come to know you before.
BLODEUWEDD	Put aside past doubts. Let this reunion Seal a new marriage between us.

LLEW   I believed you cold, uncaring.
                I didn't know you could weep
                And blur those bright eyes with tears of longing.
                Why did you keep from me till now this tenderness?

BLODEUWEDD   I was given to you my Llew as bounty,
                As a captive, without choice or say.
                You didn't learn to love me before you took me
                Or worry about winning me over. In this fort
                You have weapons and suits of burnished armour
                That cost you battles and blood to win.
                You look at them. You remember the each occasion
                Of their taking. Each one a token of your prowess
                And the pain they cost you. But me?
                I cost you nothing, not a second's sacrifice
                And that's why you've never sought
                To see the dents, the scars that line my heart
                Nor the marks of battle beneath this breast.

LLEW   You are my wife. I hope through you
                To found a race to rule Ardudwy. I wanted
                To love you as a father loves the mother of his sons.
                What greater love than that could a man dream of?

BLODEUWEDD   I was a wife to you before I was a girl.
                You demanded the fruit before the flower opened
                But I'm the woman of flowers, Blodeuwedd.

LLEW   Woman of flowers, teach me then
                How to fight my way past the petals
                And bury myself like a bee in your core.
                I too, my love, am alone in this world.
                I was a stranger to my own mother's arms.
                She cast me from her womb before my time
                Then persecuted me. In my young life
                I'd never tasted a kiss before yours,
                Nor a girl's arms around my neck.
                I never knew a brother or sister's tenderness.
                I have such longing for your love, girl.
                Teach me how to love you in your way

	For shouldn't love attract love And one heart fire another? My wife, my world, Why do you keep yourself from me?
BLODEUWEDD	I don't my love, I've never Kept any part of me from you.
LLEW	You gave your body, but kept your soul.
BLODEUWEDD	I gave you my trust. You're the only one That I have on this earth. What would I do If you were killed, leaving me without a mate?
LLEW	Was it true what Rhagnell said about you weeping?

(*She is silent.*)

	Blodeuwedd, look at me. Answer me. Why don't you answer?
BLODEUWEDD	The day you left me Despair almost broke my heart. I feared That never again would I see you alive.
LLEW	Was your love for me so great?
BLODEUWEDD	I've got no family but you.
LLEW	Half my soul, now I know your love, From now on life will sing to me sweetly. We'll make a family and a future in Ardudwy. Young saplings will grow in this oak's shadow. We'll be like a sheltered orchard Our love a palisade around us Keeping out the chill winds of loneliness. My wife, you'll be an exile no longer. I'll be your kith and kin. And unless I'm killed …
BLODEUWEDD	If you were killed?
LLEW	Don't be afraid. Killing me isn't easy. I'm fated that my death Is unlikely by the hand of any man.

BLODEUWEDD   You're reckless and neglectful.
                These details often slip your mind
                But my care for you makes me ever mindful.
                Share this secret with me, so that my heart
                Need never again be weighed with worry.

LLEW   It's a secret that I shouldn't share with anyone.

BLODEUWEDD   I'm not anyone Llew. You love me.

LLEW   I love you. Even more now than when I left.
                When I was with Math I asked him
                How he and my uncle Gwydion created you.
                He instructed, Gwydion foraged and fretted,
                Beaded sap and dew, collected scents,
                Wreathed together leaves and light
                And called on untried spells to turn that essence
                Of things wild and beautiful and primal
                Into woman. Into you.

BLODEUWEDD   In catching all those elements, they succeeded.

LLEW   Hearing Math's tale I was in awe of you
                And realised I'd been given the greatest gift of all.
                Oh yes, I love you Blodeuwedd. Doubly so
                Now that I know the secret of your making.
                And I'll gladly tell you my secret too.

BLODEUWEDD   Tell. Everything. Trust me.

LLEW   A full year must be spent
                Making the spear which is to strike me.
                It may only be fashioned at the time
                Of Sacrifice at Sunday Mass.

BLODEUWEDD   You're certain of this?

LLEW   Quite certain.
                Neither can I be killed inside a house
                Nor on my horse. Nor with a foot upon the ground.
                I have to stand on a water trough
                That is set beside a river. Positioned so,

	And struck in the back with the poisoned spear,
	I could be killed.
BLODEUWEDD	Such a fate should be easy to avoid.
LLEW	Many a time, Blodeuwedd, I wished my own death.
	But now I've a new taste for life. Love grows,
	Like an oak, strengthened by life's storms.
	Beneath its great branches flourishes
	Family, home, estates and kingdom.
	Our love, fair lady, will provide Ardudwy
	With security and strength

Enter Rhagnell.

RHAGNELL	Master, Mistress... there's food prepared.
LLEW	I'll come. Let's feast today
	As if at a wedding. I left here
	Three days ago with a heavy heart.
	I return today to a new found joy,
	Greater than any I've known. This day
	Has unfurled like a flag above my fortress, for
	I've found at last the meaning of a wife's loyalty. (*Exit Llew.*)
BLODEUWEDD	Rhagnell, I thought of killing you.
RHAGNELL	Yes Lady.
BLODEUWEDD	Then why didn't you betray me?
RHAGNELL	You're a woman, so am I.
	Another woman's secret is safe with me.
BLODEUWEDD	I can't understand humankind. You act
	According to loyalty and honour.
	Perhaps you love me?
RHAGNELL	You're innocent, like a child.
	And like a child, destructive, petulant.
	To know you is to feel sympathy for you.
	I was given to you as your handmaiden.
	As long as I live I'll be loyal to you.

BLODEUWEDD	Forgive me. I know you're wise My only wisdom is to want And seek with all my skill whatever pleases me. Will you be my messenger to the Lord of Penllyn?
RHAGNELL	Of course.
BLODEUWEDD	Tell him this: He's to make a spear of steel and poison And its fashioning must coincide With the Sacrifice at Sunday Mass. He must take a whole year in its making. When that year is up he is to return here And meet me at the foot of Cyfergyr hill. Go, hurry, that no one sees you.
RHAGNELL	Is that all?
BLODEUWEDD	That's all.
RHAGNELL	If he asks about you?
BLODEUWEDD	Tell him how happy Llew is, and that today He's returned here in love with me more than ever. (*Exeunt.*)

ACT THREE

SCENE ONE

CAER ARIANRHOD, ARFON

Enter Arianrhod.

ARIANRHOD   I had a troubled dream. I walked through snow,
             Frozen hard. Treacherous. Wind buffeted me.
             And there, ahead, a broken shape. But alive, moving.
             A bird. I called my man. What is it?

GWYDION   (*Calling from off*) Arianrhod...!

ARIANRHOD   A goshawk. Levering itself on one broken wing
             Its head turns, beak open, to hiss a threat.

GWYDION   (*Calling from off*) Arianrhod...!

ARIANRHOD   It stared at me, with burning golden eye,
             It rose, puffed out, lifting itself on one crooked wing,
             Splayed feathers extended like fingers
             Then it leapt from the snow...and laughed at me.

Enter Gwydion.

GWYDION   It's me. Your sister your brother, your darkness.
             Bearer of woe and bringer of your pain.

ARIANRHOD   And then I realised.
             Gwydion still haunts me. But no longer Llew.
             My outcast son has disappeared from my dreams.
             I don't see him anymore.
             But you ...

GWYDION   Me?

ARIANRHOD   You plunder my very thoughts. You steal from me.
             It's your game, to leave me broken, empty.
             Did you steal my cub in the dark of night?
             Were you the gale that carried off my kestrel chick?

40

GWYDION	No. I've stolen nothing from you.
ARIANRHOD	You have. You stole my happiness. My youth. You know you did. And then you stole for him. You and he turning up here in the guise Of poor shoemakers. Tempting me down to the boat Where your wares were set out. You furled Seaweed around my foot and magicked it into leather Shaped to a perfect sandal. I marvelled at your skills.
GWYDION	Yes, we worked a perfect ploy... look there my lady! My young apprentice, the arrow pulled on his bowstring D'you see what he's aiming at?
ARIANRHOD	Oh, that tiny wren! That's flitted onto the prow...
GWYDION	His arrow will split the bird between its rump And its wing. Fire the arrow lad...There! Are you impressed with his threading skills my lady?
ARIANRHOD	He's a lion with the truest hand I've seen.
GWYDION	Lion with the True Hand! Llew Llaw Gyffes. D'you not recognise me Arianrhod? Now you do! And you've just named your son! And then the other time when I magicked the hubbub Of an army attacking your fort. Soldiers shouting Horses galloping, swords and shields and screams And you in a panic thrust weapons into my hands And the hands of my young squire, not looking To see who we were. You'd armed your son!
ARIANRHOD	Get away from here Gwydion. From my lands, And from my dreams. If I could banish you forever...
GWYDION	No more than you can banish spring scents or foul air You're cursed with my presence. There'll be no peace. But it's not me making your dreams empty and arid. You're growing old now. Your horizons are drawing in.
ARIANRHOD	Old before my time. Deserted by you all. Dishonoured. And I disown you all. You, our dead brother, and Llew.

GWYDION   The disowning maims your soul, not mine.
           And Llew is happy. A complete man at last.
           With a wife he loves and a family to build.
           His future will be full of warmth and laughter
           While you wither away, a forgotten husk.
           Farewell then sister. I'll let you contemplate
           Life's losses in your fort's waking tomb
           And perhaps across the still air of Snowdonia
           Some nights you'll hear the strains of young laughter
           From Ardudwy. I go. And only the far-off sounds
           Of my voice will return to agitate you. (*Exeunt.*)

ACT THREE
SCENE TWO

CYFERGYR HILL, THE WOODS, MUR Y CASTELL, ARDUDWY

Enter Blodeuwedd and Rhagnell.

A few moments later, Gronw enters.

GRONW   I've come Blodeuwedd.

BLODEUWEDD   To the minute, brave soldier.
                        Before the sun breaks over Cyfergyr hill.
                        Don't hold me Gronw.

GRONW   I've thirsted a year for a taste of you.
                        Suffered too long an absence from your arms.
                        And you tell me not to hold you.

BLODEUWEDD   The Llew's collar still grips,
                        I've come here now straight from his arms.

GRONW   And into mine?

BLODEUWEDD   Across his corpse.
                        While he lives, don't touch me
                        In case your aim should falter. Is that the spear?

GRONW   I worked on it for a year, on Sunday after Sunday
                        At the hour of Sacrifice. This weapon cost dear:
                        A soul's perdition lies in her point.

BLODEUWEDD   Do you fear that? There's the route home to Penllyn.
                        You can choose.

GRONW   Don't mock me woman. Your fierce beauty
                        Is the fate I chose. Sunday after Sunday
                        Until this moment. A vast year yawned
                        As if unending since I last saw you.
                        Roses withered, berries died,
                        Leaves fell. Sun and moon scrawled
                        The months in slow inscriptions.

My days stood still
Refusing to move with the seasons' shifts,
Skewered by the imprint of those lips.
The furnace of your kisses honed the steel of this spear.

BLODEUWEDD   Gronw, you had an easier year than I did.
You indulged your craving, gave your longing lease
Without having to bite back sobs and stifle tears.
My heart lived in hiding night and day.
I detested the weight of his flesh
Pressing on my breasts, erasing your impression.
I'll say no more; I'll talk tonight –
Tonight, tomorrow and every other tomorrow,
And I'll be free! But now's the time to strike.

GRONW   What's our plan? My men are in the woods.

BLODEUWEDD   On that wooden trough Llew shall be killed.
The minute it's done, summon your men.
Then we'll unite Penllyn and Ardudwy.
You, Rhagnell, go, tell my husband
That I'm waiting for him here near the bank of the Cynfael
Under Cyfergyr hill. By the goats' watering place
And remind him that as I promised him last night
I'll share some news with him.

Exit Rhagnell.

GRONW   Will he come?

BLODEUWEDD   Why shouldn't my loving husband
Come to his wife?

GRONW   And what was last night's promise?

BLODEUWEDD   A hint that will bring him scurrying here.

GRONW   How shall I kill him?

BLODEUWEDD   It won't be hard.
I'll hide you here in the trees' shadows.
He can't be killed while his feet are on the ground.

	He must be standing on a water trough
	Within sound of a river. When you see him here
	Standing on top of this trough, rise
	And spear him through the back with the poisoned barb ...
	Then sound the hunting horn, and seize your prize.

GRONW   Will you get him to climb the trough?

BLODEUWEDD   Don't fail with your blow; And I won't fail
             To get him on this trough.

GRONW   My blow has been aimed this last year
             And I'll not fail. His death is not
             The goal. Beyond his corpse lies your kiss.
             That's the assurance that guides my spear.
             Only a long life, Blodeuwedd, will quench
             The thirst that's parched my soul these twelve moons.
             How long this year's been. How short I see
             The years that are left to live.

BLODEUWEDD   How interesting it will be
             To remember this day in a year's time.

GRONW   Will Ardudwy accept a new lord quietly?

BLODEUWEDD   Why not? Violent means, executed quickly
             And cleanly, yield the easiest spoils.

GRONW   I heard that he's popular with his people.

BLODEUWEDD   What's popularity? A whim. You kill him
             And his wake will become your welcome.
             Quick, hide yourself my hunter. The Llew comes.
             Join your will with mine, to urge him
             Up on this trunk. Then you'll strike.
             After that we'll laugh, and live as we like.

Gronw retreats into the shadows.

Blodeuwedd waits.

Enter Llew.

LLEW   You're up early, lady.

BLODEUWEDD   The sunrise drew me out
                    Like a rabbit to lap at the dew.

LLEW   And like a rabbit you ventured out barefoot.

BLODEUWEDD   I always prefer to be barefoot. Would you
                    Make me a shoe, as you did for your mother?

LLEW   My mother wouldn't brave the outdoors barefoot.
                    She sent servants with her foot measurements.

BLODEUWEDD   Is that the time you killed the wren
                    With a spear?

LLEW   Not a spear. No one could transfix
                    A wren with a spear. But a cobbler's needle,
                    On an arrow. With that I did.

BLODEUWEDD   A needle of course. How stupid of me.
                    Tell me how you killed the wren. Tell me.

LLEW   Gladly. But first, shouldn't you tell me
                    Why you summoned me so early from my bed?

BLODEUWEDD   The wren's story first.

LLEW   No. Your story first.
                    Why did you call me here from the fort?

BLODEUWEDD   And then the killing of the wren?

LLEW   I promise. So what is your secret then?

BLODEUWEDD   You're so impatient. Didn't I tell you last night?

LLEW   You told me that you'd keep some joyous news
                    Until today, to celebrate the anniversary
                    Of my return from Math's court.

BLODEUWEDD   Have you been happy this last year?

LLEW	How could I not have been? Your trust Was a nest to me. You've been civil and sweet, No longer a wild bird trapped in a cage.
BLODEUWEDD	You still fear wild things, my Llew?
LLEW	My mother was wild. She persecuted me. She taught me fear. I grew up Not knowing who my own father was. I hated all things wild. They're cowardly And base. They stalk and strike from behind. But you've been my walled and cultured garden, That makes me safe. This is the first year I've not feared a traitor's dagger in my back.
BLODEUWEDD	Now you've confounded all your mother's curses.
LLEW	Each one she named. There was another.
BLODEUWEDD	What was that? You've had a name; Despite her you've had weapons; you've had a wife. Aren't you free now of your mother's wrath?
LLEW	Only when you give me the best news of my life.
BLODEUWEDD	And that news?
LLEW	Dare I hope? The glorious news That through you I have a son and heir.
BLODEUWEDD	And that would break your mother's hold on you?
LLEW	My mother abandoned me. My birth sullied her. I was Her degradation and the focus For all her hatred towards the world. She cut me off from mankind, sundered me From the carefree days of boyhood; I was forbidden the very trappings Of young manhood; a name, arms, a woman. I had to fight against her for my sense of self. Gwydion was like a father to me. You're now my wife.

	King Math gave me lands for my princedom.
	I've known the cares common to men; through you
	This year, I've known caring. Love. The nightmare
	Has receded and is often forgotten. But Blodeuwedd
	If I once saw, cradled against your breast
	A boy, my heir, the last link in that cruel chain
	Would fall away and I would glory
	In being a life-giver. In fathering a future.
BLODEUWEDD	Without that you won't be happy with me?
LLEW	Without that, I'll be content. With that my love
	And gratitude would serenade you endlessly.
BLODEUWEDD	But that wouldn't be a song in my honour.
	Just a serenade of triumph over your mother.
	It hurts me Llew that you can't once look at me
	And say – "You, you're enough for me."
	If you said that –
LLEW	I'll say it when a boy rests in your arms.
BLODEUWEDD	What fateful words! Listen to my secret.
	I have an heir for you, here.
LLEW	You know for certain?
BLODEUWEDD	As every woman knows.
LLEW	Oh, my queen! Let the fates make it a son.
BLODEUWEDD	He is a lad, I swear it.
LLEW	I never dared to think
	Your words last night hinted at this.
	My cup is brimful. If death itself should strike now
	I'd not begrudge it!
BLODEUWEDD	Death strike now? Aren't you charmed against
	Any attempt your mother might make to kill you?
LLEW	My mother's wrath counts for nothing if I have an heir.
	What will he be like? Imagine it my love.

BLODEUWEDD	Keen in his kissing. I can see him now, His lips eager for my lips. A hunter. His horn will startle the stags And Ardudwy's halls will echo with his prowess.
LLEW	I'll teach him his father's skill at games.
BLODEUWEDD	Will you teach him to throw a spear, and a needle?
LLEW	And how to row and how to make a shoe for his mother So she doesn't have to go barefoot in the dew.
BLODEUWEDD	And will you tell him the story of shooting the wren?
LLEW	I can picture him now, a three year old In your lap listening to Gwydion's tales. How the old wizard will make the boy smile With his story of our boat outside Arianrhod's keep.
BLODEUWEDD	Tell me that story, as if I'm your heir. Let's pretend that this trough is the boat. Where did Gwydion stand?
LLEW	Here, mid-deck, Peering down at my mother's foot.
BLODEUWEDD	And you, the nameless youth Stitching the shoe leather, where were you?
LLEW	There in the stern.
BLODEUWEDD	Did your mother look at you?
LLEW	Yes. Long and hard with lips pursed.
BLODEUWEDD	But without recognising you?
LLEW	Gwydion had woven a spell. She was beautiful, standing, her foot on the boat's rail. Upright, and proud, a princess.
BLODEUWEDD	Like this? Facing out to sea? And then?

LLEW   It was spring. Ten yards offshore
                    Stood a stone sea-wall. From one of its crannies
                    The wren appeared, skipping and darting
                    In and out of the crevice. It flitted
                    Then came to rest on the boat's prow.

BLODEUWEDD   Here? Show me how it stood.

LLEW   Look, like this ...

Gronw emerges from the shadows, his spear poised.

LLEW   There stand Gwydion and my mother
                    Myself here. A moment of stillness.
                    The water's surface shimmering, not a sound ...
                    The wren perches. He raises one wing
                    Like this ... his head downwards. That second,
                    The needle weighted in my fingers ...

BLODEUWEDD   A needle, not a spear ...

LLEW   I aimed at him ...

GRONW   Like this.

Gronw drives the spear into Llew's back.
Llew falls with a scream.
They look at him.

                    Is he dead?

BLODEUWEDD   He shuddered, struck his head on the ground,
                    And then was still. There's no sign of life.

GRONW   The poison won't fail. Not even Gwydion
                    And all his sorcery can undo this death.

BLODEUWEDD   Come, the new heir ...

They embrace.

BLODEUWEDD   He is a lad, I swear it.

GRONW   I never knew a better ending to a story ...
                 Yes, he's dead.

BLODEUWEDD   A man dies so easily.

GRONW   Look, the sun's breaking through the trees.

BLODEUWEDD   Let's wait a minute.
                 I can't believe his death happened so simply.

GRONW   Let's go and take the fortress.

BLODEUWEDD   A scream, then gone.
                 Will it be like this when it's my turn?

GRONW   Come Blodeuwedd. This isn't the time to ponder ...

BLODEUWEDD   But wait. What shall we do with this?

GRONW   I'll send soldiers to bury him this afternoon.
                 Come girl. We'll go to the fort, to secure
                 Our new estate. We must move, come now! (*Exeunt.*)

A moment's pause, then Llew's stricken body stirs slightly.

LLEW   I'm dying. Gwydion. Where are you? Gwydion!
                 I'm dying. Uncle! Help me!

Llew struggles to his feet.

Exit Llew.

ACT FOUR
SCENE ONE

CAER ARIANRHOD, ARFON.

Enter Arianrhod.

Enter Gwydion.

ARIANRHOD   You. Back here. You
Who left me to wither to a windblown husk.

GWYDION   I'm here for Llew.

ARIANRHOD   I heard that Llew was slain. Outside his fort in Ardudwy.

GWYDION   He was. His body left beside the river Cynfael
Or so we thought. But when I went
To retrieve that body it wasn't there.

ARIANRHOD   The wolves and kites and maggot-pies work quickly.

GWYDION   But then, a month ago, I heard a strange tale
Of a half man half eagle in the forest near your fort.
Curiosity drew me there. I found it
Perched on a branch, its flesh rotting, its feathers dropping.
Dying slowly, being eaten alive by blowflies.
Was it some instinct that made it drag its carcass
Back to its mother's home?

ARIANRHOD   I also heard his fortress, princedom and Blodeuwedd
Are now possessed by another.

GWYDION   Give us shelter Arianrhod.

ARIANRHOD   No lands, no wife, no son, no heir.

GWYDION   Give us shelter Arianrhod.
I can heal him.

ARIANRHOD   Why should I help you?

GWYDION   You're his mother.

ARIANRHOD	You're his father my sister brother.
GWYDION	I can make him whole again.
ARIANRHOD	You're his father Gwydion. You know this to be true.
GWYDION	Perhaps I am, perhaps I am not.
ARIANRHOD	Have you forgotten that stormy night When we were Math's young charges, You, me and Gilfaethwy? Have you forgotten? The two of you came to my bed. You'd been drinking and fighting. Gilfaethwy was in some frenzy Made wild by mead and lust and anger. He raped me. Or tried to. I used all my strength To fight him off. My own brother was an animal He hit me and hurt me but failed to penetrate me. Sleep stayed his violence. I lay numbed and hurting. Then you, you Gwydion, my sister brother climbed upon me Pinned me down and forced yourself inside me. Ever the coward, you stole your brother's Exhausted prey. You are Llew's father.
GWYDION	I remember nothing of that night.
ARIANRHOD	My life was changed forever Gwydion. Since that night my thoughts are run through With darkness. I've trusted no-one. Loved no-one. Not you my brother, and not Llew our son.
GWYDION	I'll heal my son without your help.
ARIANRHOD	Go! Go to Annwn to rot with the corpse Of your monstrous brother Gilfaethwy! (*Exeunt.*)

ACT FOUR
SCENE TWO

THE GREAT HALL, MUR Y CASTELL, ARDUDWY

Enter Blodeuwedd and Rhagnell.

RHAGNELL   A traveller came from the north today
            From Nantlle. He told us a strange story.

BLODEUWEDD Nantlle. I don't know any of these places.

RHAGNELL   Not far from Caer Arianrhod.

BLODEUWEDD And the story?

RHAGNELL   Answer me first. Have you seen Llew's grave?

BLODEUWEDD No.

RHAGNELL   Has Gronw?

BLODEUWEDD I don't know. I don't think there is a headstone. Why?

RHAGNELL   There's comfort in a grave. It signifies a death.
            Headstones on enemies' graves give the living a sounder sleep.

BLODEUWEDD You needn't worry. Gronw's a sound enough sleeper.

RHAGNELL   Is his sleep as sound as Llew's by the goat trough?

BLODEUWEDD What do you mean?

RHAGNELL   That's where Llew Llaw Gyffes was killed wasn't it?
            But I've not heard anyone say they buried him.
            Perhaps one of his soldiers stole the body?
            Strange that Gwydion never came from Caer Dathl
            Nor one of Arfon's bards to mourn above the grave.

BLODEUWEDD You suspect that Llew Llaw Gyffes is alive?

RHAGNELL   That's what I was told by the man from Nantlle.
            Gwydion fought against the poison for Llew's life.
            And saved him. The man had seen Llew with his own eyes

In Caer Dathl's stables, or so he claims.
He's alive today, and well again. He's on his way here.
He has a score to settle with Gronw Pebr.

BLODEUWEDD   Ha! I've been expecting this.

RHAGNELL   You've been expecting it, lady? Since when?

BLODEUWEDD   Since a year ago this day. Since the lands
Of Penllyn and Ardudwy were united.

RHAGNELL   You believe it's true? If that's the case
Gronw must make his escape, yourself too.

Enter Gronw.

BLODEUWEDD   Did you hear Gronw?

GRONW   I heard everything. My captain's heard the same.
He urges me to flee to Penllyn. Llew approaches
With three hundred fighting men. We have forty.
Some of those were pressed into our service
Here in Ardudwy. I can't trust them with my life.
And those that I do trust... I've looked into their eyes
They have the honour of Penllyn etched in their hearts
And also families and lands back home.
I'll not ask them to die here, on my whim.
I'll face the Llew alone when he comes
To reclaim his territory. You two must flee.
But I must stay and do what honour decrees.

BLODEUWEDD   It's not that honour's re-awoken in you Gronw.
It's that passion's died. A year's a long time.
That wild edge has blunted. I've felt it.
Novelty pales. Ardour wanes. To you passion
Was a dalliance, a stolen ecstasy.
To me it's life. It's what I am.

GRONW   And I am what I am.
There's always a battle between duty and passion
You said you're a cousin to the wolves
You live to devour, to scavenge and to mate.

55

You have needs. They rule you.
I have lust too. But I can curb it, and set it aside
When obligation demands. Go Rhagnell.
Collect your mistress's possessions
Ready for your journey to Penllyn.

RHAGNELL Is this the end of our time in Ardudwy?
My days here are over?

GRONW Yes. Your duties here are done. You must leave.

RHAGNELL If that's your decision, I'll go. (*Exit Rhagnell.*)

BLODEUWEDD You don't have to listen to that dull beat
Of duty. I've taught you better.
I'll go. But you must come with me...

GRONW Where?

BLODEUWEDD Not to any fort. But to the woodlands.
We'll follow the river to the dark caves
Of its source. That's my empire.
Come with me Gronw! We'll be wild forever.

GRONW Don't touch me woman. The hour's come.
We must part. You have a journey ahead of you.

BLODEUWEDD I won't leave here without you.
I won't leave you alone in Gwydion's hands.

GRONW Your husband lives. He'll be here now.
You can't stay.

BLODEUWEDD I can't go to total strangers.
They'll kill me without you.

GRONW I've told you. I'm going to face the Llew.

BLODEUWEDD There'll be no one staying behind, but you?

GRONW I won't be alone for long. I'll soon have company.

BLODEUWEDD I'll wait for Rhagnell to return.

GRONW	I wouldn't be too surprised To see her arrive with Gwydion. After all he gave her to you as a maid.
BLODEUWEDD	Rhagnell was never devious. She's a loyal woman. She was our go-between, remember?
GRONW	Remember? Too well. Do you want to stay, with me?
BLODEUWEDD	Yes. I'm frightened. But I don't want to leave you. You don't even have your weapons, Shall I fetch A sword, a shield? Don't you intend to fight?
GRONW	It's not my turn to strike. Not this time.
BLODEUWEDD	And you'll fall to your knees in front of him? He can't forgive. I know my Llew.
GRONW	I can forego his mercy. I'll settle for The stab of his spear.
BLODEUWEDD	Do you want to die?
GRONW	How long it's taken you to read my mind.
BLODEUWEDD	What do you think you'll achieve by your death?
GRONW	A final hour of freedom.
BLODEUWEDD	I don't understand you. Out there are horses, ready, saddled to go, And freedom in their stirrups. Why don't we go?
GRONW	Freedom's here. Here with you.
BLODEUWEDD	With me? O, my Gronw. I misunderstood. But no, I see now ... Your freedom is us dying in each other's arms And we crown a short life's love with this last defiance.
GRONW	My freedom doesn't lie in your arms.

It's in having you here when my end comes
And in choosing death, your sister, before you.

BLODEUWEDD   You want to disown me? Blame me
For making you a murderer? Plead before Llew
That a woman's wiles were to blame for what you did.
Is that how you'll gain your freedom?

GRONW   You needn't worry. I don't expect your death
Will save my life. I've only minutes
Left to live. Your husband, woman,
Is coming and so is my death. I choose that.
It's in that choice that I find my freedom.

BLODEUWEDD   So your freedom is to escape from me?

GRONW   I can't escape from you except through death.
The poison of your kisses circulates in my blood.
Why should I live on? To taste for a lifetime
That which I've already experienced?
You were right Blodeuwedd. Passion's fire
Turns to embers. You sate the body till surfeit sets in.
And then staleness, and shame, follow indulgence.
Your love is a grave, not a future. No child
Will laugh in those arms; there's no cradle in our keep.

BLODEUWEDD   How d'you know that? Llew thought he was fated
Not to bear children with me. That fate
Even if true, does not extend to me.

GRONW   No matter now. There is no future.
In the deep of night there's the sound
Of a lunatic crying, howling on the breasts
Of darkness and chewing on dirt, urged on
By the mocking screech of an owl.
I lost the paths of humankind, to follow
Torches to a quagmire, and I sank. I sought
To grasp at a star; a clawing bat clung to my face.
Today a bolt has struck me, and I woke up.
I see Penllyn again. I see my childhood there.
Then I see myself as I am now. Oh, filthy!

58

And your stare spearing me. I'd rather
His sword than your kisses.

Llew and Gwydion enter.

GWYDION   Walking through an open door as if to a banquet
And the lord and lady awaiting us with their welcome.

Llew takes hold of Gronw and pushes him to his knees.

LLEW   Where are your men, traitor?

GRONW   All dispersed.
I alone struck you. You needn't seek others
On whom to vent your wrath.

Llew ties Gronw's hands.

GWYDION   And here's the handsome heir, a son of Gronw Hir,
But now without followers, a captive, no spear to hand.

GRONW   Lord, you don't need to tie me; I stayed
To do your will. I'm ready for your revenge, standing
As free as you yourself stood on the goat trough.

GWYDION   That's true nephew. I knew his father,
And the fortress at the lake's edge. Untie him,
We must respect the wishes of a man condemned to die.

LLEW   I won't let him escape. Only a cord of flax binds his arms;
He bound me with the tethers of a wife's lies.

GRONW   What do you want lord?

LLEW   Your life.

GRONW   You have a right to that. I'll yield it gladly.

LLEW   You spent a whole year plotting my death
Another full year you took possession of my bed,
My fortress, my princedom and this half-human harpy
Who once passed as a wife. It's not for that either
That I want your blood, rather because you heard

	The greatest secret of my soul, and laughed.
	You mocked at my misfortune – you ridiculed
	The confession of a man ensnared by love
	Your treachery cut you from mankind;
	The mark of the forest is on you. You can't live.

GRONW   How d'you want to kill me?

LLEW   Uncle Gwydion, what shall we do with him?

GWYDION   We'll decide what to do with him presently.
             There'll be another body on the banks of the Cynfael.
             But this time there'll be no laughter, and no physician.

GRONW   No tears either, but a welcome to death.
             I'll come back among mankind by passing through
             Those common gates that claim all mortals.
             Thank you, sir. And you... (*To Blodeuwedd*)
             I curse the day I met you.

BLODEUWEDD   My man of magic, you've travelled far today,
             But you don't want me to greet you.
             Or offer you mead to quench your thirst?

GWYDION   Your husband's already tasted your poison.
             You've brought death and misery to those around you.
             Let's show her Llew, what we found by the stream.
             The wiser the servant, the quicker
             They are to pre-empt punishment.

BLODEUWEDD   What wisdom? What servant? The only
             Servant that I could call my own was Rhagnell.
             She's not deserving of any punishment.

GWYDION   As we approached the fort we found
             A body on the riverbank, drowned...
             Wild dogs were already feeding on it,
             Trying to drag it out of the water.

*Gwydion drops a blood soaked garment at Blodeuwedd's feet, it is Rhagnell's.
Blodeuwedd clasps the garment to her.*

BLODEUWEDD   No!

GWYDION   Rhagnell's chores are all done now.

BLODEUWEDD   Fear of exile killed her.

GWYDION   No. Cowardice killed her.
              There's no steel in woman-kind.

BLODEUWEDD   No steel? But there's blood. So much blood!
              She was a mother to me – the only one
              Who didn't want to use me. She taught me things.
              She could forgive me. She understood.

GWYDION   She also understood that punishment
              And revenge and death were imminent.

BLODEUWEDD   My happiness alone is deserving of your punishment.

GWYDION   Happiness? That's what's foremost in your mind? What of
              Poison, treachery, mayhem, luring a husband to his death.
              Some little details that are not to everyone's taste.

BLODEUWEDD   Am I the first unfaithful wife?

GWYDION   I'm not saying that. Your sort is one of many,

BLODEUWEDD   You're a sorcerer Gwydion, steeped in learning,
              You're strong and bold enough to challenge nature
              To toy with it and battle with the power
              Hidden in the rocks. Why?
              To satisfy what? You chose Llew as your heir
              You wanted to make him worthy
              Of Math's throne, a future king of Gwynedd,
              And a father to a line of princes no doubt.
              His life was blighted by his mother's conditions,
              But you, the oak wizard, master of creation's codes,
              You made it your great mission to reshape his destiny.
              Then you raped the woodland to flesh him a wife.
              Me. So I became your captive and his slave-girl
              You gave me this form to tend on him,
              To soothe away his cares, help him forget his birth-lot

	And see if I could give him children. Tell me Gwydion, wasn't that your grand design?
GWYDION	Is it a violation to ask a wife To bear her husband a son?
BLODEUWEDD	Thank you, wizard. But it was fated that Arianrhod's son Should never have a wife of woman born, He feared too that he would never sire a son. He wouldn't submit to his fate, Not him, nor you. I was caught, a pawn, In your tinkering, to trick his fate. Is it wrong of me at least to be true To my instinct? I begged him, This youth not meant for love, to look at me And take me once for what I was. But he struck a song of jubilation for his son And told his last story to his heir and future hope; He wouldn't leave his dream of tomorrow To share the today of my empty heart.
LLEW	Gwydion, it's true. She has been wronged. She doesn't deserve to die as that other does.
GWYDION	Do you say that? I don't believe it!
BLODEUWEDD	Gronw has chosen to die. Rhagnell is dead. Why should I live?
LLEW	I came here bitter, intending for you A savage punishment. I see now That you've always been a creature to pity.
BLODUWEDD	You fought against your fate. I fought mine; We've both battled against what must be.
LLEW	That's why I can forgive you. No rational soul could love like you.
BLODEUWEDD	One tried. I gave him to you as your heir.
LLEW	And he's chosen death to escape from you.

BLODEUWEDD	And your jealousy needs to claim his life. Because he could love, and he set my love on fire. What will you do without me, poor husband, You know you'll have no other wife of woman born?
LLEW	I'll accept my destiny And make a nest of my sorrows.
BLODEUWEDD	Oh, I can hear your mother laughing long and loud.
GWYDION	I wonder? You don't hear her sobbing in the night.
BLODEUWEDD	Your hearth will be so empty, your bed so cold.
LLEW	We're all exiles. The world's a cold hearth. I'll join the army of bitter souls.
BLODEUWEDD	Here's a destiny that'll please your mother. From now on you'll never know love.
LLEW	The love I could achieve, I gave to you. I put my life in your hands. You betrayed it.
BLODEUWEDD	So I could gain a life myself. Take your revenge.
LLEW	I can't. You may walk from here, freely.
BLODEUWEDD	How gracious of you. And I'll go where? To my family? To my loved ones? To my lover?

Gwydion stands behind the kneeling Gronw.

GWYDION	This creature? He doesn't love you now. He fears you Despises you even. Tell her Gronw.
GRONW	I feel nothing. With her I experienced everything I was on fire with her. We loved. We lived. We lusted. Not now. Not ever again.
GWYDION	No. Not ever again. He expects death. He lived outside our code of honour. He crossed the gods. And the gods are on our side.

BLODEUWEDD	I hate you Gwydion. I hate your gods.
GWYDION	I'm a god myself. In that I create life. And I can kill love. So easily. Right here.

Gwydion takes a knife and cuts Gronw's throat.

BLODEUWEDD	No! I loved him Gwydion.
GWYDION	You're avenged my Llew.
LLEW	Am I? With everything around me dead or dying.
GWYDION	Honour and revenge are satisfied. Life will go on. But this demi-creature, Half woman, half animal, what shadow world Will welcome her? What land of lost souls?
BLODEUWEDD	I'll go to the woods. Maybe I'll rot away. Maybe I'll live a while. Unless you destroy me With the same speed with which you made me.
GWYDION	I won't destroy you. Nature will do that for me.
BLODEUWEDD	You forget that I am nature, and nature Regenerates. It's greater than man's devices. It will outlast you all. I'll go back To the kingdom of the senses I'll create mayhem in men's dreams And sunder the foundations of your ordered world.
GWYDION	Listen before you go. In the woodland There's a bird which is fearsome, like you. And like you, loves the night. Its shriek, Like your laughter, is an omen of death. Between it and the other birds there is hatred. Your sojourn among men was not happy. Go to the darkness, to the company of owls, To the rites of the moon and the hollow trees. Now as you cross this threshold, And blink from the sun, your mocking laugh

Shall become an owl's shriek, and never again
In daylight will you show your face.

Blodeuwedd smears herself with blood from Gronw's corpse.

BLODEUWEDD   To the black earth and the twisted trees
Where I'll waste away, like all life does.

GWYDION   And you'll be an exile forever.

BLODEUWEDD   In that I won't be alone,
My tortured wizard and my abject husband....

She smears the blood on Gwydion and Llew.

BLODEUWEDD   But first I'll go to Arianrhod's fort.
I might even have earned some welcome there
And she might get the companion that she's craved.

She runs from them unleashing a blood-curdling scream.
The scream turns into an owl's screech.

A white owl in flight.

Gwydion wipes the blood from Llew's face as they stand over the bloodied body of Gronw.

EPILOGUE

CAER ARIANRHOD, ARFON

The sound of waves crashing onto the shore.

Arianrhod is cradling something in her arms.

The screech of the owl turns into a baby's cry.

END

The Royal Bed

by Siôn Eirian

An English Language Adaptation of Siwan by Saunders Lewis

Theatr Pena / The Riverfront Co-Production in association with the Torch Theatre

The Royal Bed was first performed at The Riverfront, Newport on 11th February 2015 with the following cast:

SIWAN	Eiry Thomas
ALIS	Hannah O'Leary
GWYLIM	Francois Pandolfo
LLEWELYN	Russell Gomer
SOLDIERS	Ian Buchanan
	Eirian Evans
	Richard Balshaw
TROBAIRITZ	Buddug Verona James (Voice)
	Delyth Jenkins (Harp)

Director	Erica Eirian
Assistant Director	Brenda Knight
Designer	Holly McCarthy
Lighting Designer	Kay Haynes
Sound Designer	Mike Beer
Musical Director	Buddug Verona James

Production Manager	Ian Buchanan
Stage Manager	Julie Towson
Assistant Stage Manager	Eirian Evans
Technician and Relighter	Daniel Sawyer
Set Construction	Adjacent Education Project
Costume Supervisor	Deryn Tudor
Scenic Artist	Reva Callan
Design Assistant	Christina McConnell

Marketing Officer	Megan Merrett
Producer	Ceri James

Theatr Pena is grateful to the Welsh Assembly Government and the Arts Council of Wales and the following Theatr Pena 2014–15 Supporters for supporting this production:

Acanthus
Kate and Peter Carroll
Sir Alan Cox, CBE
Julie and Bryn Davies
Ian and Sonia Donald
Barbara Francis
David Groves
Hugh Hudson-Davies, CVO
Julian Mitchell
Fiona Peel, OBE
Meic Povey
Ann and Michael Robinson
Dr Tamsin Spargo
Prof. Elan Closs Stephens, CBE
Stephen and Mary Walsh
Maggie Weakley
John and Judi Wilkins

THE ROYAL BED

CHARACTERS

SIWAN

ALIS

GWILYM

LLYWELYN

SOLDIERS

ACT ONE

The royal chamber in the tower.
It is past midnight.

SIWAN   The music's over now.
There – the last lantern's been put out.

ALIS   The big lantern up there's still going strong.

SIWAN   What a moon. Such a light night.
We hardly need these candles ...
What time is it Alis?

ALIS   I heard the watch calling midnight as I came here.
Shall I take the crown ma dame?

SIWAN   Yes. Put it away in the chest.

ALIS   Wasn't the dancing on the green a delight?
You could see the knights from France were enjoying it all so
    much ...

SIWAN   Now this gown. I can't wait to be free of it Alis.

ALIS   Yes ma dame.
I heard one of the Frenchmen say how strange
It was to see the courtly dances of Aquitaine
Here on a castle green in North Wales.
They didn't realise how you'd brought
The graces and manners of Toulouse
With you to the wilds of Wales.

SIWAN   They shouldn't be surprised at that.
Half the English court are Frenchmen.
The new Welsh nobles have French blood.
And tonight we're celebrating a pact
Between France and Gwilym's Brecon
Which will be sealed when his daughter marries my son.
The French knights knew the significance
Of the contracts we made this evening.

ALIS	Why didn't you dance ma dame?
SIWAN	With that heavy crown, weighing on me so? That great silver gown billowing around me? Even for the French dances I'd need far lighter Dress than that. My duty tonight was to take the throne In my Prince's absence.
ALIS	But no one can dance the French steps As beautifully as you. You'll have to lead the dancing Come your son's wedding, just as you've done When all your other children married.
SIWAN	Yes. I'll dance at Dafydd's wedding. A dance to celebrate his golden future. I'll dance for Dafydd.
ALIS	Shall I let down your hair now, And comb it before you go to bed?
SIWAN	Do that Alis. The crown pressed into my head And made my temples ache. I'd like you to comb my hair. I'll sit here for you.
ALIS	(*Sings*) Le roi Marc était corracié Vers Tristran, son neveu, irié; Da se terre le congédia Pour la reine qu'il ama.
SIWAN	Not that song Alis. Not tonight.
ALIS	It's Marie de France ma dame. You taught me the words.
SIWAN	As my mother taught them to me. But Tristan and Isault is too sad a story for tonight.
ALIS	She sings the kind of song I understand. That moves me. Not like our bards.

Their poetry's too cold and too clever
For a country girl like me.
(*Sings again*) En sa contrée en est allé,
En Sud Galles oû il fut né ...

SIWAN   Let Tristan and Isault rest Alis ...
And finish my hair.

ALIS   Was Tristan a Frenchman then?
How was he born in South Wales?
En Sud Galles oû il fut né.
Brecon's young lord, Gwilym Brewys, has French blood then?
When I was looking at him out there tonight I was thinking of
    Tristan.

Siwan gives Alis a resounding slap.

Oh ... *ma dame*! What did I say?

SIWAN   Have you finished with my hair girl?

ALIS   Look in the mirror ma dame.
You'll see two braids, just like Isault's ...
My lip's bleeding where your ring caught me.

SIWAN   The taste might teach that tongue of yours a lesson.
The wine I left outside, did you give it to the doorkeepers?

ALIS   Didn't you see them as you came here?

SIWAN   They were both sleeping soundly,
One on either side of the door.

ALIS   The doorkeepers sleeping!
Shall I go wake them?

SIWAN   No. Let them sleep.
Tomorrow's May Day.

ALIS   It's already May Day.
And already the lads and girls
Are out there in the groves, dancing.
Hands held around the may pole

	Then they'll be pairing off, the couples
	Creeping away. I don't suppose
	That many of them will reappear before dawn.
	Oh, those country boys know how to have fun too
	Ma dame.
SIWAN	Have you ... been with boys Alis?
ALIS	Of course. The first time was when I was fifteen.
	You've never been out under the may pole?
SIWAN	I was a King's daughter. And at fifteen
	A mother myself, to a little prince.
	I gave my young womb to political imperative
	Like every royal daughter.
ALIS	The trees are so still now. I can't even
	Hear the sounds of the sea. It's at its far ebb.
	If I were a Princess, on a May Day eve like this
	I'd put all my duties aside.
SIWAN	You don't know what you're saying Alis.
	Take your candle to your room, go to bed.
	I won't sleep for a while yet.
	I'll knock on the floor if I need you.
ALIS	Good night then. God be with you ma dame. (*Alis exits.*)
SIWAN	(*Sings*) Pour la reine qu'il aima.

Gwilym appears.

GWILYM	My Lady ...
SIWAN	Gwilym!
GWILYM	Siwan – I've been waiting, outside the keep.
	What made you detain her such a time?
SIWAN	Today, at sunrise, Henry, King of England,
	My brother, sails for France.
GWILYM	Yes? What of it?

SIWAN	You're a hot blooded young man ...
GWILYM	Twenty five, and a father to four daughters.
SIWAN	I still see you as that brash young upstart Captured, carried here wounded from battle For us to subdue and to nurse ...
GWILYM	Why tell me about your brother? What if he is travelling to France?
SIWAN	That's why I kept my maid here the while.
GWILYM	To keep me away?
SIWAN	No. The implications Gwilym. My significance. I bind two kingdoms. A King of England And a Prince of Gwynedd. Your coming here now, is no trifling matter. What if one of Gwynedd's Royal Council Saw you crossing the green and entering this keep? What if my Prince was to learn of this? With my brother away in France He'd have a free hand to wreak his vengeance In whatever way he wanted. The implications Gwilym.
GWILYM	No one saw me. Don't worry. And your guards Were sleeping. Did you drug their wine?
SIWAN	A prudent precaution, knowing how reckless you can be.
GWILYM	Don't forget – I'm almost one of the family here. Your daughter's my step-mother And my daughter will soon marry your Dafydd. That gives me some right to come and go ...
SIWAN	Not in the dead of night. Not in the royal bed, like this.
GWILYM	You want this marriage – your Dafydd To my daughter - more than anything. I know.

SIWAN   Yes. I want it. But it's the Prince's decision.
         He's fifty-seven. He wants a grandson.
         Allying with you and Brecon secures our borders,
         And a child from that alliance would also secure
         Llywelyn's bloodline.
         Longevity runs in Llywelyn's family.
         If our Dafydd and a son of his inherit that trait
         This kingdom could be secure for another century.
         One lesson that Llywelyn continually tries to teach me
         Is that success is bred from patience.
         Yet I find patience such an elusive virtue.

GWILYM   And what lessons have you taught him?

SIWAN   You're married, a hearthful of daughters,
         Don't you know that a wife has nothing
         Worth teaching her husband?

GWILYM   I do know you say that mockingly.
         I'll show you one wife - a Prince's wife
         Who's consulted as a prime minister,
         Who's the court's chief ambassador
         And who walks the halls and makes heads turn
         As if she were Helen of Troy ... My lady?

SIWAN   Perhaps that's a form of escape for me.
         I inherited a passionate, restless nature,
         From my father.
         To keep myself sane I occupy my time, like a man,
         With my husband's stratagems, his statesmanship.

GWILYM   Do you know what they say about you
         Down in South Wales?
         That Gwynedd, thanks to your influence,
         Has become a French princedom.
         All your children have been given away
         To a French nobleman in marriage.
         You've almost changed your Welsh Prince
         Into an adopted Frenchman.

76

SIWAN	The only thing that forges real change in a man Is love. Are you telling me That Llywelyn loves me as you do?
GWILYM	You're the first successful politician That I've found to be intelligent and intuitive Siwan.
SIWAN	The unruliness of passion is anathema to statesmanship Only once did I allow my heart To rule my head in such matters.
GWILYM	And when was that, my lady?
SIWAN	When I suggested the union Of Gwynedd's heir To Gwilym Brewys's daughter. Of mine and yours.
GWILYM	An inspired suggestion.
SIWAN	A desperately bad suggestions If Dafydd doesn't sire a son.
GWILYM	You astonish me Siwan.
SIWAN	Why?
GWILYM	You know why I came here to your court.
SIWAN	To finalise the arrangements for that wedding.
GWILYM	And why do I want to see that wedding happen As much as – if not more than – you do?
SIWAN	Because you have no male successors. Four girls won't secure the future of Brecon. And we border on Brecon. Our northern princedom Dwarfs your swathe of lands. Just as to your south you're dwarfed By Hubert de Burgh's South Wales territories. Make an ally of us – and you'll sleep more easily

	And your small kingdom will swell in stature
	Like a cub protected by the great lion's paw.
GWILYM	O, Siwan – I didn't come here to talk politics.
SIWAN	Talking politics with you Is a form of defence for me.
GWILYM	How is that?
SIWAN	It keeps my thoughts from other things.
GWILYM	Are you frightened of some other truths?
SIWAN	Not frightened of the truth – But of hearing it spoken perhaps.
GWILYM	Do I frighten you Siwan? Is that it?
SIWAN	Not you. The things I'm really frightened of Are within me. And you awaken them.
GWILYM	They're the very things That make life so sweet.
SIWAN	They can make life bitter too If they're suppressed and hidden away – I buried them somewhere deep in my soul Knowing that I dare not set them free, Not even acknowledge them in my life here As Llywelyn's princess and political partner. Because I had to make that choice Between my natural passions And stately protocol. Yes, I'm bitter.
GWILYM	You've guessed then why I came here To arrange the wedding.
SIWAN	You don't understand do you That politics and pleasure should not mix.
GWILYM	I wouldn't call my longing for you a pleasure.

SIWAN	Is your flatterer's tongue faltering?
	Or do you mean to say that your longing
	For me is becoming burdensome?
GWILYM	One thing I didn't come here to do
	Was to exchange jibes.
SIWAN	That wasn't a jibe.
	I'm ten years older than you.
	Dafydd, the son in law I'm giving you
	Is almost as old as you.
GWILYM	I was only ten years old,
	At my father's wedding in Hereford
	When I first set eyes on you, Princess,
	As you led your first daughter, a child bride,
	To be my father's second wife,
	And the crowd in the church garlanding
	Your path with rose petals.
	I didn't speak to you then – I couldn't.
	My heart was in my throat.
	I gathered up a handful
	Of scented rose petals,
	And they were my pillow that night.
	Not that I slept.
	My mind was restive, hungry ...
	I didn't see you then until I was brought here
	In manacles. My wounds were light –
	But I became feverish.
	You came to my bed, surrounded by your maids.
	Walking towards me as I'd seen you in Hereford.
	Was it the fever?
	Or was it my breathless excitement
	That made me sweat and lie atremble
	As you knelt over me, placing your lips on my mouth?
SIWAN	You fainted. You frightened us so.
GWILYM	But you knew that my wounds weren't serious.
	It was that kiss. It was fated,
	Like Isault's kiss ...

SIWAN   Gwilym, ssh ... Not that unhappy tale.
               Tristan and Isault have haunted me this evening.

GWILYM   I'll talk of happier things.
               When I'd recovered, I stayed awhile.
               We'd go riding along the mountain passes
               Stopping on some sunlit verge to drink wine.
               And there was singing and dancing in this fortress ...
               The halls of Gwynedd's court were
               As bright as any in Aquitaine.
               Then your kisses turned from courtly greetings
               To a hotter, sweeter foretaste
               Of this tryst tonight.
               Do you remember when you first kissed me
               With your mouth on fire, greedy ...

SIWAN   And the very next day Llywelyn returned.
               With your ransom paid.

GWILYM   He's got a knack of returning
               At the wrong time.

SIWAN   We had a week of discretion
               And keeping distance.
               Then you left.

GWILYM   You see. And that's why I've returned.
               My daughter's marriage to your Dafydd
               Was agreed by me, so that I could be here now,
               To claim you, make love to you Siwan.
               Of course, you knew that.

SIWAN   Did I dare know it? I didn't think
               You'd give your daughter's hand
               And your castle in Builth as dowry
               Simply to open the way to my bed.

GWILYM   I'd give my whole kingdom
               For this night in your bed Siwan.

SIWAN	All your worldly wealth? Like Saint Francis. Sanctity and sensuality are two poles Of the same madness. They both make men Forsake reason and caution.
GWILYM	I heard that Francis as a young man Was a gambler and a squanderer. I like men who gamble, with money and with fate Who can lose and still cock a snook At life and luck. If Francis was ever such a lad He's the Saint for me.
SIWAN	I'll pray to him on your behalf Asking him to guard you from ill-fortune.
GWILYM	But not tonight. Fortune's with me tonight. If I lose my luck and lose your love Then I'll plead with Saint Francis.
SIWAN	You love danger too much. That reckless bravado of yours Makes me fear for you.
GWILYM	You have to take me as I am Siwan. Since I was a child I've been in my element hunting, fighting Accepting dares. That's how you squeeze The grapes of experience till your mouth Runs with the tang of their juices.
SIWAN	Am I one of those bunches, Ripe on the vine?
GWILYM	Your taste will be sweeter Siwan. More exquisite, even more heady.
SIWAN	Did you mention this to anyone At my brother's court?
GWILYM	Who would I tell?

SIWAN	And you told nobody that I suggested This Easter as the time to meet To make the wedding arrangements?
GWILYM	Perhaps I mentioned that. Perhaps I told Hubert the Chancellor. Such details Interest him. Why?
SIWAN	Hubert de Burgh is a venomous viper of a man. And my husband was with him yesterday. What if Llywelyn comes back here With Hubert's insinuations nagging in his brain?
GWILYM	If Llywelyn suspected anything He's a wily enough statesman To let me deliver my castle as dowry Before unleashing any angry accusation. I know the Prince of Gwynedd.
SIWAN	That's more than I can safely say And I've been married to him for twenty five years. A Prince and statesman can be as impetuous as the next man.
GWILYM	Why talk of him now? You promised this night to me.
SIWAN	I do give you this night. I give you myself, my heart, my body In this royal bed. Here, now, I'm yours Gwilym Brewys.
GWILYM	And your love? Do you give that too Siwan?
SIWAN	I don't know yet. Tonight, yielding willingly is enough. Tomorrow, who knows. Perhaps I'll be in love with you tomorrow. But by then tonight will be over And we'll wonder if there can be another.

GWILYM	I'll wait. You summoned me tonight You put the opiates in the guards' possets.
SIWAN	I did that. My own hand. Tonight's my gift to you.
GWILYM	And why Siwan? Why all this for me?
SIWAN	Because you remember how things first taste And how that first taste is all, before it fades. Because you laugh at danger And life's frightening fragility. Because your excitement is mine to take And your ecstasy is mine to give. Because it's now the eve of May Day.
GWILYM	Your bed is beckoning Siwan.
SIWAN	Come to the window first Breathe in this scented night air. I'm giving all my senses full rein tonight. And look at that moon over Anglesey Gwilym.
GWILYM	D'you hear those sounds, like horses in the distance?
SIWAN	Hill ponies, panicked by something, stampeding?
GWILYM	Those steeds are shod, I tell you.
SIWAN	There's nothing now.
GWILYM	No. Not now. But my ear Is attuned to the sound of hooves. I'm hardly ever mistaken.
SIWAN	What was that?
GWILYM	That was a dog. Somewhere by the fortress gate.
SIWAN	Gelert.
GWILYM	What?
SIWAN	It was Gelert. Llywelyn's hound. I'm certain of it.

GWILYM   No. He's taken Gelert with him.
          To do some hunting on his journey home.
          What a dog! I saw it once
          Running down a stag, bounding along the crags,
          Defying death, above the abyss ...

SIWAN   I know Gelert's bark. I heard Gelert out there.

GWILYM   You heard a dog. But not Llywelyn's hound.
          Siwan, my love. The candles' flames are flickering low
          And this royal bed begs us to make bold use of it.
          Let me take you before the light dies.

SIWAN   Sshh! Listen!

GWILYM   I can't hear anything ...

SIWAN   People over by the gates, people moving,
          Someone's arriving, coming in ...

GWILYM   It's your imagination. Your pretty ears
          Are flattened back like a frightened cat's.
          Why are you suddenly so nervous?

SIWAN   No – Listen! There!

GWILYM   The fortress gates, yes, opened and closed.
          The sentries are probably changing shift.

SIWAN   When the guard changes Gwilym
          No one opens the main gates.
          Something's afoot. And now, men running ...
          Look, look! Torches moving through the dark.
          Towards this keep.

GWILYM   What's happening?

SIWAN   Dear God – what is this?

GWILYM   Soldiers are surrounding this tower.
          You're right. Something's going on ...

SIWAN   Your sword. Where's your sword?

| GWILYM | Not with me. Not even a dagger. Nothing. |
| | I'm going to see if the stairway's clear. |

| SIWAN | He's here. Gwilym! Llywelyn is back! |

| GWILYM | And tens of armed soldiers around this keep's entrance. |
| | We've been betrayed Siwan. We're trapped. |

| SIWAN | Can you get out between the window pillars? |

| GWILYM | The space is too narrow. |
| | Where are the maids' chambers? |

| SIWAN | Down next to the tower's door. |

| GWILYM | And what's above us? |

| SIWAN | The turret loft. It's locked. |

GWILYM	There's nowhere to escape.
	No move I can make.
	The Prince must be welcomed to his royal chamber.
	It sounds as if he's on his way.
	How shall his welcome be?
	Simple and sans ceremony?

| SIWAN | Come to the bed. Lie here, in my arms. |
| | I'll give myself to you now my love. |

Llywelyn and soldiers rush in.

| LLYWELYN | Take him. Tie his hands and arms. |

| GWILYM | You won't need to do that. |
| | I've no dagger or sword. |

LLYWELYN	Tie him up I said. Stand him here.
	Gwilym Brewys. I caught you once before,
	In battle. As a prisoner of war
	You were free to walk this castle's halls,
	Your wounds were nursed ...
	This is how you repay me!
	Making Gwynedd's queen a harlot

	And myself a cuckold, to be ridiculed In the courts of France and England.
GWILYM	Now there spits the rhetoric of wounded pride. I've loved a Princess, who's a married woman, But so do hundreds of noblemen. Such things are as much part of our lives As jousts and tournaments. You caught me in your bed. Very well – Exact your penalty, Make me pay for this indiscretion. You're already promised my castle in Builth as dowry And your son is to take my daughter. Now for this – take more of my lands, Of my wealth – take anything you want.
LLYWELYN	This indiscretion? Make you pay! You French lords are lousy jesters. When I beat you in battle that cost you A third of all you owned. The whole Of your possessions wouldn't come close To paying for this infamy tonight. Oh yes, I'll take your castle in Builth. I'll also take your life.
GWILYM	That's more than you would dare. Your anger, my Lord, is clouding your common sense. Every lord in France, in England and the Marches Would turn against you, and take up arms to challenge you If you dared kill me. That action Could ruin Gwynedd.
LLYWELYN	If the Pope himself and the whole Of Christendom vowed to rise against me – I'd still take your life.
GWILYM	Oh! This isn't righteous anger Or wounded dignity. This is jealousy! Siwan, my lady, what other Princess In the whole of Europe has a husband who ...

86

LLYWELYN	Shut him up men. Gag his insolence.

Gwilym is gagged.

SIWAN	My Lord. May I ask a question?
LLYWELYN	You?
SIWAN	Yesterday you bade farewell to my brother The king before he set forth for France.
LLYWELYN	What of that?
SIWAN	Was it then Hubert de Burgh who told you of this?
LLYWELYN	And if it was, would that Make your whoring any less heinous?
SIWAN	He owns strategic shires to the south of our kingdom. His power's expanding, his wealth growing.
LLYWELYN	This is no time to discuss Hubert's estates.
SIWAN	Hubert is close to taking the rest of Glamorgan And soon he'll have a kingdom in South Wales To match the size and strength of Gwynedd here.
LLYWELYN	Ma dame – I don't hear your counselling. I see only this treachery This desecration of my bed, my wife ...
SIWAN	Gwilym Brewys has no male heir. Who but he can stand between Gwynedd And Hubert de Burgh? Between Hubert's ambition And the security of our princedom, Dafydd's future throne ...
LLYWELYN	Aye, no one but he. Yet you'll not persuade me. You'll not have your way.
SIWAN	If you kill Gwilym, his territories will fragment And Hubert de Burgh's might will border our own. Was it to help Hubert's aspirations That you rushed home tonight?

LLYWELYN	Ma dame your concern for me is touching.
SIWAN	It's not easy to set aside A quarter of a century's politicking.
LLYWELYN	Easy though to cast aside your clothes To toss your purity to the swine.
SIWAN	I've wronged you. Of course I have. But now I'm arguing for your kingdom's sake, Our son's inheritance Llywelyn.
LLYWELYN	Are you claiming that such thoughts Were in your mind as you took This scoundrel to the royal bed?
SIWAN	I'm asking you to pause, to think. Putting a pair of cuckold horns on your head Isn't a reason for letting your teeth be drawn.
LLYWELYN	Not even adultery's enough for you. Your shameless mocking Is insult upon injury Siwan.
SIWAN	I'm a Frenchwoman. And a King's daughter. Your Welsh moral strictures Aren't part of my upbringing Llywelyn.
LLYWELYN	A Frenchwoman best served by a Frenchman eh?
SIWAN	I'm trying to protect your life's achievements From one night's rage. Gwilym Brewys's life Is vital to the security of This kingdom's southern borders.
LLYWELYN	Gwilym Brewys's life is what you're desperately trying to save.
SIWAN	Yes … Yes.
LLYWELYN	So, then – he will die.
SIWAN	And your kingdom, the future We've been building for Dafydd?

LLYWELYN	To hell with the kingdom and with you. I've lost my wife tonight. Now you can lose your lover.
SIWAN	You daren't kill him.
LLYWELYN	Take him to the dungeons.
SIWAN	My brother – he'll come back from France ... The King of England, Llywelyn ...
LLYWELYN	This vermin will hang. Like a common brigand.
SIWAN	Gwilym!
LLYWELYN	Yes. He'll hang.
SIWAN	Gwilym!

Siwan runs to Gwilym.

LLYWELYN	No – stay away from him.

Llywelyn strikes her hard across the face. She cries out.

> I never thought I'd hit you ...
> Take him from here.
> Take her to the tower loft.
> And lock her up.

ACT TWO

A bare loft in the tower.
The sound of hammering and wood assembling outside.
Alis enters.

ALIS   Have you woken ma dame?

SIWAN   No. Because I haven't slept.

ALIS   All night long? Not slept at all?

SIWAN   I'm not used to an iron clamp and chains
            Around my leg. Or being tied to a wall
            Like a fairground bear. The chain's heavy Alis.
            Feel its weight – the weight of a Prince's anger.

ALIS   The weight of his disappointment ma dame.
            His disappointment far outweighs his anger.
            Does it hurt your leg?

SIWAN   It hurts my dignity so much
            That I hardly feel the pain in my leg.
            Before now I've ordered men to be manacled
            And chained without even guessing
            At the indignity of it.

ALIS   The Prince says you're only to stay in chains
            Until today is out.

SIWAN   Why today and not tomorrow?
            What will change today?

ALIS   I can try to ease your discomfort.
            I've brought some wine.

SIWAN   Did he send you here?

ALIS   Yes. To attend to you, and do your bidding. I'm free
            To come and go – the guard's been told.

SIWAN   That guard's a mute. All day yesterday
            I didn't see a soul. Only that mute beyond the door.

ALIS	A mute carries no tales.
SIWAN	And can't act as a go between. That's why the mute was chosen. So why are they allowing you to come to me now? Has <u>he</u> changed his attitude towards me?
ALIS	Will you have some wine?
SIWAN	This wine's sharp. But it'll quench my thirst. Today's the third of May. Isn't it?
ALIS	The third, yes.
SIWAN	Two days, two nights. This cell's deathly silence Makes May Day eve seems years away. Did you ever sleep alone in a bare room Alis?
ALIS	No ma dame. I'm not a princess. I've never even had a room of my own.
SIWAN	The solitude of this cell is different. It's a world Where silence reigns. Where speech is redundant. That dumb guard ... These dumb stones.
ALIS	But you never were a talkative one ma dame.
SIWAN	I know. But it drives me to distraction, Not knowing what's happening Beyond the silence of this cell. What time of morning is it Alis?
ALIS	The sixth hour.
SIWAN	The sixth since midnight. Add twenty four to that And another twenty four. I've been in this tower Almost sixty hours. I once listened to a learned monk Explaining that time doesn't exist In eternity. I hope he's right. Counting each hour's passing is as maddening To the mind as the sound of that hammering outside. It started sometime before dawn.

ALIS	You haven't slept for three days ma dame. You haven't eaten any of the food that's been sent Io you. No wonder your mind's agitated.
SIWAN	So, why were you sent here Alis?
ALIS	I told you ma dame. To see if you needed anything.
SIWAN	And the Prince himself sent you?
ALIS	Yes ma dame. He did. Otherwise The guard wouldn't have let me pass.
SIWAN	There's some mystery here. He told you To see to my needs. Are you allowed To carry messages for me?
ALIS	I don't know. He mentioned nothing about that.
SIWAN	That's my only need. The only service You could render me. What is that incessant hammering Out on the green?
ALIS	Some military construction – I'm not sure ...
SIWAN	You must have seen them working As you crossed the yard to come here.
ALIS	I didn't pause to get a proper look. A little more wine ma dame?
SIWAN	Go to the window and look out. This chain Stops me short of seeing outside. If my father the king had known I'd be tethered Like some animal for baiting ... So what are they building?
ALIS	It's hard to see properly from this window.
SIWAN	Don't lie to me girl. You can see perfectly well From there. I've looked through that window myself Countless times. So tell me.

ALIS	Ma dame – don't ask me. Please. I beg of you, let me leave you now.
SIWAN	What's wrong with you. You're shaking. Calm down – and tell me what's happening out there.
ALIS	A gallows ma dame. A gallows.
SIWAN	Gallows?

(*She laughs*)

> Well done Llywelyn. That's my punishment.
> Your rage is greater than I imagined.
> Alis, don't cry – if that's to be my fate ...

ALIS	Not you ma dame. It's not for you.
SIWAN	What?
ALIS	The gibbet ... is for Gwilym Brewys.

Siwan falls in a faint.

> Ma dame? Ma dame?
> Oh Ma dame.

Alis raises the goblet of wine to Siwan's lips.

> Take a little more wine.
> There we are.
> You frightened me my lady.

SIWAN	I'm ashamed of myself.
ALIS	It's not surprising. What with not having slept or eaten. And the shock of ...
SIWAN	Was I in a faint for long?
ALIS	A few seconds. Why?
SIWAN	The hammering's stopped. Has anything happened out there?

ALIS	Nothing ma dame. It only stopped a moment ago.
SIWAN	That's good. Whatever happens, I want to be aware of it. Have the soldiers finished? Go and look.
ALIS	Yes. It's finished.
SIWAN	How was he sentenced Alis? By the Court of Law? Or by the Prince himself?
ALIS	Yesterday. At about mid-day. The Court was alive with rumours all morning. Bishop Cadwgan had been summoned by the Prince, And he'd suggested that the young Lord Had come into your rooms through witchcraft.
SIWAN	No doubt the Bishop was trying to placate Llywelyn With a comforting explanation. And who knows. Witchcraft it may have been. There's something other worldly in such frantic longing. That's why real passion is such a rare visitor to our lives.
ALIS	Your temple's bleeding ma dame.
SIWAN	A little loss of blood might cool me down. After the Bishop's visit?
ALIS	The Royal Court was assembled.
SIWAN	Was my son Dafydd there?
ALIS	No. He'd been sent away to Cardigan. That same morning.
SIWAN	I'm glad. And what was resolved by the Court?
ALIS	It's said that Ednyfed Fychan Did plead for the young Lord's life, So as not to antagonise England And the Marcher lords. That plea failed. The Prince Wouldn't listen. Not even to a plea For a beheading rather than a hanging.

	He wanted a common thief's execution for Gwilym In front of a crowd of ghouls, rather than A death more fitting to a nobleman. Ednyfed Fychan was shocked by the sentence. Even when the courtiers filed out He still sat there, ashen, and silent.
SIWAN	And when was the verdict announced?
ALIS	Yesterday afternoon ma dame. The hanging's set for early morning, now, Before the hour of mass. A crowd's been gathering for two hours or more Outside the fortress gates.
SIWAN	Does he know?
ALIS	Yes.
SIWAN	When was he told?
ALIS	Bishop Cadwgan was with him for an hour Last night. He's with him again now.
SIWAN	And have you heard any news about him? How is he?
ALIS	No one's allowed near his cell. Not even Near the dungeon sentries. The knights Who rode up here with him are also imprisoned. But last night ma dame, after the Bishop left his cell, I walked quietly past the dungeon tower. I heard him singing.
SIWAN	What was he singing Alis?
ALIS	Marie de France. "La roi Marc était corracié Vers Tristran, son neveu ..."
SIWAN	Have you ever seen a hanging?

ALIS	Of course ma dame. Many times.
	Brigands and robbers. Have you?
SIWAN	No. Never. Strangely enough.
ALIS	With robbers, it's a big show
	Which attracts more people than do fairground fools.
	It's best when the man is petrified
	And has to be pushed to the top of the ladder.
	His hood's pulled down. The priest recites the *Ave*,
	Offers to hear his confession. After that
	The hooting and the shouting of the crowd takes over.
	I saw a pirate once, in Borth, joking
	As he climbed the ladder
	And toasting the cheering crowd
	Then doing a jig as he dropped
	And the rope sprang taut.
SIWAN	How long do they take to die?
ALIS	Some a long time. Others quickly.
	Some still twitch after hanging for a full half hour
	But it depends how the ladder's thrown
	And on how the noose has been knotted.
SIWAN	Who throws the ladder?
ALIS	The soldiers or the executioner.
	I've heard it said, if the rope is tied very tightly
	And the man jumps, he'll kill himself
	In a couple of seconds. I never saw that happen.
	A girl I knew did. She said the leap
	Pushed the tongue back into the throat
	And up behind the nostrils. Before the feet stop kicking
	The backbone's snapped in two.
	But usually you see these robbers swinging wildly
	In the noose, and the life's squeezed out of them
	Slowly, and the face turns blue.
SIWAN	Holy Mary – let him leap like Gelert.

Drum.

Go to the window Alis. Tell me what's happening.

ALIS   Oh – Ma dame. Your lover's there now …
                I never thought I'd see a lord go to the gallows.
                He'd come here to give away his daughter's hand
                And he's so young, so much living left …
                More than once he made me laugh out loud, chucked me
                    under the chin, flirted with a courtly kiss …
                In Gwynedd's Court there are many who'll mourn after him.

Drum.

SIWAN   Stay at the window girl – or I'll break this chain.

ALIS   I don't know if I can …

SIWAN   I'm not going to swoon a second time.
                I won't even shed a tear Alis.
                I want to go through these minutes with him
                And be brave for him.
                Take up your place.

Drum.

ALIS   The soldiers have formed a guard around the gibbet.
                Crowds are no better than herds, or packs
                Of mindless animal. Look at those faces.
                How the human face changes when demons distort the mind.
                The choir and church procession
                Are going past now.

SIWAN   Saint Francis, let him keep his hands free
                So that he can leap.
                Saint Francis, you loved the wild wolves,
                Please help my little wolf.

Drum.

ALIS   There are so many in now, it's a crush.
                Right back to the fortress walls.
                The soldiers are pushing them back, to keep the gallows clear.

Drum.

The Court Officers of Gwynedd are arriving.
Ednyfed Fychan leading them out.

SIWAN   Is <u>he</u> there?

ALIS   The Prince? The great chair's not out on the green
And I can't see him with them.
He can watch it all from his rooms
Up there, out of the rabble's way.
Ednyfed is arranging the ranks of noblemen.
He's taking charge, preparing the stage for the show.
That's why the crowd's quieter now.

Drum.

The soldiers are making a passage, flanking
The condemned man's path.
Each with his spear and shield
Keeping a clear space for the last slow walk.

SIWAN   I can't pray. I don't know how to pray.
I'd willingly strike a bargain
With any saint who'd listen.
I'd spend a life in prison, if only
He be allowed to leap!

ALIS   The six French knights who came here
With Gwilym Brewys have been led out
Still manacled. I imagine they'll be allowed
To take the body back to Brecon.
And the Bishop of Bangor is reading the last rites.
Now he – Gwilym Brewys – turns towards the crowd …

SIWAN   How does he look?

ALIS   He's in breeches, a shirt. He's barefoot …
The noose is around his neck …
One of the Prince's stewards is holding the other end …
Like some animal on a tether.
But his arms and hands are free.

SIWAN	Free? He can leap? He'll be able to do that … Does he look frightened?
ALIS	No … He looks Strangely untroubled. The crowd are fascinated by him. The last minute now … The time's come.

Drum.

SIWAN	All the saints, if you can pray, pray for him.
ALIS	He's shaking hands with Ednyfed Fychan and Gwynedd's Council, One by one – like a lord greeting his guests At a banquet. He's got a word For each one, and they're laughing … Now he's kneeling in front of the Bishop. The crowd's silent. Astonished. Even the Court dignitaries are staring in disbelief.
SIWAN	Yes?
ALIS	No one's moving now – except Gwilym. He's testing the ladder. Even feeling the noose … Easing it around his neck. He's bowing – a farewell bow. And … Now he's ascending the ladder, like a ship's Captain to the prow. He's standing Confident and unbowed …
SIWAN	This hour … The hour of his dying – Amen.
ALIS	The executioner's not moving, not laying A hand on that ladder …

Suddenly a shout from Gwilym.

GWILYM	(*Off stage*) Siwan!

A second's silence.

SIWAN   (*Quietly*) Is that the end?

ALIS   But the leap he made, that leap!
               The rope whipped taut like a fishing line.
               The ladder was knocked sideways
               Scattering the councillors …
               Now his body's stock still,
               Still and limp, hanging there.
               The crowd's moving away. Starting to disperse.
               For them the show's over. It's been a let down.
               What do they care about a widow down in Brecon?
               Or a Princess imprisoned here,
               Distraught and eaten up by anguish.
               Pain's a leprosy.
               It cuts off the sufferer from the rest of the tribe.
               It's the one dark corner
               In their bright and babbling world.
               You lot, yes, go dance, go laugh,
               Go seek some further entertainment.
               Go crowing your Welsh bravado …

Sounds from outside the loft room.

               Ma dame!

Llywelyn and soldiers enter.

LLYWELYN   Take that chain and fetter from her leg.
               Her degradation's done. Over.
               (*To Siwan*) I wouldn't dare would I? I wouldn't dare?

SIWAN   From the depth of this hell in my heart, I curse you
               Llywelyn.

ACT THREE

The royal chamber in the tower.

Alis enters.

ALIS   Sir, my Lord, my mistress is getting ready.
                She'll be here with you shortly.

LLYWELYN   I sent my son to escort her here.
                Is he with her?

ALIS   Yes Sir. This is the first time my mistress
                Has seen him since his wedding.

LLYWELYN   A whole year, yes … Is she well?

ALIS   As well as can be expected, after
                A year's imprisonment.

LLYWELYN   Confinement, not imprisonment. She had everything
                She asked for, apart from her freedom. Two maids
                Waiting on her every whim, a courtyard for fresh air …

ALIS   Yes. Everything except her freedom.

LLYWELYN   And by that, you're implying – what?
                Tell me girl.

ALIS   A command Sir?

LLYWELYN   A command, yes.

ALIS   Your son, Prince Dafydd, got married.
                His mother wasn't at the wedding.
                She didn't lead the dancing afterwards. All that day
                She was left on her own with her thoughts.

LLYWELYN   My son married Gwilym Brewys's daughter,
                As arranged. How could we have allowed
                Your mistress to have danced
                In the hall of Brewys's widow?

ALIS	The wedding dance is only a ceremony.
LLYWELYN	For a royal family life itself Is often only a ceremony.
ALIS	She's changed my Lord.
LLYWELYN	Everybody changes. Even our memories change. Anger changes. Vengeance changes. How has your mistress changed? Tell me what your observed.
ALIS	This whole year gone, she's not struck me once.
LLYWELYN	Have you deserved to be struck?
ALIS	(*Laughs*) I don't know Sir. Striking servants is done from habit, not desserts.
LLYWELYN	And she's let that habit slip?
ALIS	My Lord, before her confinement She was young at heart.
LLYWELYN	That's not what was on your mind girl. Tell me what was.
ALIS	I've said all I dare Sir.
LLYWELYN	The hanging of Gwilym Brewys devastated her. Her love of life went with Gwilym into that noose. That's what you're telling me.
ALIS	That's my worry Sir. And you did ask me.
LLYWELYN	I have to ask someone. A year Without a beating has made you impudent.
ALIS	I'm not a serf or a peasant's daughter. My father was a freeman.
LLYWELYN	You're also married aren't you?
ALIS	A widow these last three years my Lord.

LLYWELYN	Forgive me. Yes. One of my retinue. He was killed in battle at Castell Baldwyn. A brave lad.
ALIS	I'd only seen him once before being betrothed to him And then, after two weeks' marriage, the war ... He went. I never saw him again. And now It all seems like some young girl's daydream.
LLYWELYN	But a daydream, not a nightmare? He was killed as we tried to scale the castle walls. I remember it. D'you remember bidding him goodbye?
ALIS	In the small hours. I heated him a cup of milk. Fresh from the goat's teat. He gave me a milky kiss, we were laughing ... He was still laughing as he joined the other soldiers. They saddled, mounted, rode away waving. We were just starting to get to know each other.
LLYWELYN	Every husband and wife Are just starting to get to know each other, Whether it's two weeks or twenty years. You're a brave one too.
ALIS	Me Sir?
LLYWELYN	You got on with living your life.
ALIS	Did I have a choice?
LLYWELYN	There isn't one brave and thinking soul Who hasn't at some point contemplated Not carrying on with life. To us all, life is a gruelling gift.
ALIS	Even for a prince?
LLYWELYN	A prince is a man isn't he?
ALIS	Are you going to say that to the Princess Sir?

LLYWELYN   Doesn't she already know?

ALIS   It would help her to hear you say it.
             Making war, laying plans and all the state's affairs
             Lie like some wide walled-off field
             Around a prince. His greatness sets him apart;
             But to us women – yes, even a woman who's queen –
             The mother's instinct is the root of our love.
             And our first born is the man who married us
             When we're girl brides. When the child in that man is lost
             The woman too loses part of her love.

LLYWELYN   Showing a weak side is to show one's humanity –
             Is that it?

ALIS   Gwilym Brewys was a child Sir. A young child.

LLYWELYN   And it's little children who enter the kingdom of love?
             I'll mull over your lessons Alis.

ALIS   My Lord, I'm only a maid. You asked me to speak.
             I learnt what I know in these royal halls of Gwynedd.
             I treasure this place, and its lord and lady.
             This lost twelvemonth, this empty husk of a year,
             Has hurt us all.
             The Pope's excommunication would be
             Child's play compared to the inner grief
             All of us have already felt.

LLYWELYN   The Pope's excommunication will yet come,
             If that's of any consequence now ...

ALIS   So the stories are true?

LLYWELYN   What rumours have you heard around the court?

ALIS   That you're going to war
             Against the King of England.

LLYWELYN   That issue is to be settled today,
             By your mistress. The choice is hers.
             A war, or the end of Gwynedd. That's why

	I called her up from the confinement of her rooms.
	The fate of Wales lies in her hands.

ALIS	Sir – here she is.

LLYWELYN	Stay nearby, in the maidservants' room. I may
	Need to call you back in a while. I hope so.

Alis exits.
Siwan enters.

SIWAN	You called for me my Lord. Here I am.

LLYWELYN	Siwan!

SIWAN	My Lord?

LLYWELYN	Siwan!

A moment's silence.

	Siwan – it's me, Llywelyn ...Siwan!

SIWAN	Llywelyn?

LLYWELYN	I need you Siwan ... Me, Llywelyn.

No reply.

	I need you Siwan.

SIWAN	You need me?
	How can that be?

LLYWELYN	Why shouldn't that be?

SIWAN	I've been a prisoner for months now my Lord.

LLYWELYN	A year to this morning.
	Oh yes – I've been counting the days too.

SIWAN	Is today May Day eve? I've lost count.

LLYWELYN	It is May Day eve.

SIWAN	Do you have to be so unfeeling towards your prisoner?
LLYWELYN	Unfeeling? What do you mean? I don't understand.
SIWAN	Today of all days – ordering me here Straight from my prison. Why did you call me?
LLYWELYN	To continue that talk between us. The talk That started and ended a year ago.
SIWAN	No, no, no. Not ever again. I can't talk about Gwilym. Show some pity my Lord. Let me get back to my cell.
LLYWELYN	I need you Siwan. I'm begging, not commanding And I didn't choose this morning to wound you. Last night a messenger came to me from South Wales. That's why I've summoned you now. God rest Gwilym's soul. Hubert de Burgh is the thorn in my flesh now. Here – that night – you foresaw this. You foretold it, like some Cassandra. All your words have come to pass, and I Must once more go to war against your brother.
SIWAN	Once more to war? Is that the Council's advice?
LLYWELYN	The Council hasn't yet been convened. I'm seeking your advice first. Then I'll consult my councillors.
SIWAN	Why my advice?
LLYWELYN	I've a right to your advice. Adultery And confinement don't lessen my rights.
SIWAN	Yes, you have a right. I gave you that right. And I can't withdraw it now. But why do you exercise your right today?
LLYWELYN	The prerogative of Gwynedd's crown Is what I'm exercising. And that crown Is now what's at stake.

SIWAN	And you're ordering me to co-operate?
LLYWELYN	If that's how you wish to see it.
SIWAN	Why d'you need to go to war again? You're almost sixty. What d'you have to prove?
LLYWELYN	I was informed last night Of William Marshall's death.
SIWAN	I've been a whole year without news, My reactions are dulled to its significance. But how does William Marshall's death Take us to the brink of war?
LLYWELYN	Last year Gwilym Brewys's lands Were placed in Marshall's charge.
SIWAN	And now?
LLYWELYN	Those lands now pass on to Hubert de Burgh.
SIWAN	Fortune comes to those who seek it. You've done your share to help him prosper – I seem to recall telling you so.
LLYWELYN	And the Earl of Gloucester recently died.
SIWAN	And his successor is his little son?
LLYWELYN	Yes. The child's guardian Also happens to be Hubert de Burgh.
SIWAN	(*Laughs*) And the little Earl's lands In Gloucester and Glamorgan?
LLYWELYN	Hubert has charge of those too.
SIWAN	Your friend Hubert grows evermore corpulent Through feeding on good luck Or a diet of very wily design.
LLYWELYN	Everything you prophesied is coming true Siwan.

SIWAN	That won't undo a death or unknot a noose.
	That night I was trying to save a life.
	Your rage made you deaf to political wisdom.
	God rest Gwilym's soul. Hubert is a viper.
LLYWELYN	His lands are now stretched from Hereford to Cardigan,
	Spanning all Dyfed, Gower, Brecon and Glamorgan.
	Gwilym Brewys and Marshall and the Earl of Gloucester
	Have all served to feed Hubert's voracious aspirations.
SIWAN	And he's Chancellor to the English crown.
	So England's court and France's are his allies.
	Dare you go to war?
LLYWELYN	(*Laughs*) It's madness I know. But how can I sit back
	Without forcing fortune? There are still lands
	To the South split among the grandsons of Lord Rhys
	Which cling to their independence, and to my
	Protection. I must show that I still have
	The strength to deserve their allegiance.
SIWAN	If you do nothing – will Hubert
	Court those weaker lords?
LLYWELYN	Yes. And then his lands.
	Would be greater than Gwynedd.
	He would be two thirds of Wales.
	His jaws a pincer closing round my northern kingdom.
SIWAN	We can't have two great Princes
	Astride this nation's land.
LLYWELYN	That's my quandary.
	That's why I need to act soon.
SIWAN	And where's my brother now?
LLYWELYN	The King's in the English Court.
	I must rally my lands to attack him
	And use that call to arms to widen the war
	Against Hubert and the Marcher lords

	For they're all arrayed against me.
	I'm now the common foe.
SIWAN	All against you? Then you dare not go to war
	On all fronts. We've always clung to a peace
	Between ourselves and the English, and the Marches,
	Whatever the bitter internal feuding within Wales.
	That was to be the great security
	That we would hand on to Dafydd our son.
LLYWELYN	But never before have Glamorgan and the South
	United under one Prince, threatening us.
	War is now inevitable.
SIWAN	War is inevitable. Yes. But when we
	Go to war it should only be
	When we know that we can win it.
	Dafydd's inheritance is at stake.
LLYWELYN	Everything you and I have striven for
	Is at stake. My crown, our bloodline,
	Wales's proud standing and secure future.
SIWAN	A year ago today you should have
	Given thought to these great matters.
LLYWELYN	A year ago today I did consider these matters fully.
SIWAN	Did you?
LLYWELYN	Here – in this room – you prophesied
	The consequences of executing Gwilym Brewys.
	Then in the Council, at the Court, I repeated
	Your warnings. I spared no details.
	They were debated. Ednyfed Fychan agreed with you.
	The Bishop of Bangor agreed. I too believed you.
	I knew that the Kingdom of Gwynedd and my crown
	Were being risked, when I hanged Gwilym Brewys.
SIWAN	May I ask you then, why you did?

LLYWELYN	It's right that I tell you why, And I will tell you shortly. But first my Lady, Matters of policy. Back to the old discipline.
SIWAN	What of England and the Marcher lands? Are there any weaknesses there now?
LLYWELYN	There lies our hope. The earls and bishops Who went on the crusades are returning.
SIWAN	Including Hubert's fiercest enemy, the Bishop Peter?
LLYWELYN	Yes. He'll be back in England Before the summer's end.
SIWAN	England's court and the Marches Will be at each other's throats. Can you delay war until then?
LLYWELYN	No. I can not – not if I hope to keep The southern lords' allegiance. If they see me Stalling now, they'll scuttle like mice To Hubert's house. I must attack before summer.
SIWAN	Would early in June be soon enough?
LLYWELYN	Perhaps. Why?
SIWAN	Let loose the southern lords now – to take The spoils from Gwilym Brewys's old kingdom And promise to join them in the despoiling soon. But in the meantime send word to England Asking the King's help, keeping the peace, the pact, Then the crusaders will return. They'll take a hostile stance Towards Hubert in Hereford, and challenge His sudden influence in Gloucester. Some of the Marcher lords Are headstrong and haughty enough to engage Hubert de Burgh in battle. His army will be Dragged hither and hither on different fronts Then you strike. His mighty Southern kingdom

	Could be a great dream that never Does become a reality.
LLYWELYN	Your advice seems sound. And your advice Is in the best traditions Of Gwynedd's measured policy making. Retaking those newly garnered lands In Hubert's kingdom would buckle again The belt of my grip on Wales. I'll follow your advice Siwan – on one condition.
SIWAN	Does the condition have to do with me?
LLYWELYN	I'll follow your advice If you return today to my table and my bed.
SIWAN	Does that imply forgiveness?
LLYWELYN	Would you accept that?
SIWAN	Forgiving is a form of overcoming. I haven't forgiven you.
LLYWELYN	For killing Gwilym Brewys?
SIWAN	I knew that his life was destined to be short. Killing him was a human response. I forgive that. But because he loved me, And because I gave myself to that love, You gave him the death Of a mountain brigand and a common thief. You opened our castle to the grimacing Cackling peasants of Arfon. You hanged him To show your hatred, to spit venom on our love Before the crowds of your subjects.
LLYWELYN	He died with dignified disdain – it was A death worthy of your love.
SIWAN	Your councillors were ashamed. Your courtiers went quiet, Ashamed of your obsessive hate.

LLYWELYN	Didn't it cross your mind Siwan That I could love you as much as Gwilym Brewys did?
SIWAN	You – you, love me? No ...
LLYWELYN	Is the chasm between us that great?
SIWAN	My Lord – I was given to you, a bride, At the age of ten. You were Already a Prince, in your thirties. Four years after that I came to your bed, The first time quivering like a frightened leveret. I was your wife and bed partner for twenty years. I gave you an heir; I gave you daughters. I took part in your Council's debates. More than once I saved you From the anger of my father, and then my brother. I was a shield between you and England's throne. I travelled to other courts as your representative. I put my shoulder behind the building Of your great kingdom. And then, Once, before my bloom faded, came a lad Who sang a song that lit a flame In my tired heart. You strung him up like some crow on a garden pole.
LLYWELYN	That's true. I regret that to this day. He had to die. But I didn't have to hang him.
SIWAN	Why then? Why? I can't live with you, I can't lie in the royal bed again Without being told why.
LLYWELYN	You can't understand why. For you, I don't exist.
SIWAN	You exist as a nightmare does. Since that day.
LLYWELYN	I know. Your Gwilym was closer to me in one way Than you were. He saw me as a person. I had to gag his mouth, to stop him Betraying my truth before you.

SIWAN	Tell me what Gwilym saw then.
	I shared that bed with you for twenty years.
	I've a right to know.
LLYWELYN	Telling you would be like baring my breast
	To your venom's barbs.
SIWAN	A year's imprisonment has blunted those barbs.
LLYWELYN	Our marriage was a political union.
	Between us – a divide of twenty five years.
	That's the common practice. That's how
	Political pacts are made. The fate
	Of countries and crowns hang on such things.
	But four years after that wedding, when you
	Came to Arfon, a vision of virginal beauty,
	My heart stopped, I was breathless, as if I'd seen the Grail.
	There was a light where your feet had walked
	And when I felt you trembling.
	Pressed against me, girdled by my arms,
	I said, I showed ... nothing. I didn't want
	To give you any cause for further fright.
	I didn't even discomfort you with a kiss.
	No cloying embraces. Nothing to make you
	Recoil from me. I held back. I was courteous,
	Even formal, in my advances. You relaxed.
	Into the familiarity of these rooms, into my company
	And I became part, a vital part perhaps
	Of your days' routine.
	I worshipped you from a discreet distance,
	From afar and without voicing my thoughts.
	And, wanting to involve myself with you more,
	I began engaging you in the affairs of my state.
	I saw your wisdom, your acumen, burgeoning.
	You impressed me so. I remember that afternoon
	You returned from England, from your father's court.
	There was the threat of invasion then.
	You were only fifteen, and Dafydd our son
	Hardly two months old. You had saved
	My kingdom, had staved off war.

That night it was you who embraced me.
I had no language to express my bliss,
I had to stop my own body from trembling ...
After that night I became ruthless
Towards this kingdom's enemies. I resolved to build
A mighty inheritance for our son. If I could,
I wanted to give him the whole of Wales.
I persuaded the Pope and the English crown
To acknowledge me as the Prince of Wales.
I constructed a great kingdom,
As a shrine to you, a monument of my love for you.

SIWAN   Llywelyn, I didn't know. I didn't know.

LLYWELYN   What good would it have done you to know.
There was a mountain range of years
Between us. I understand that too,
I'm a statesman. I don't ask the impossible.
For me, your fidelity sufficed.

SIWAN   In twenty years of living together
You never said that.

LLYWELYN   In twenty years of living together
You never saw that.

SIWAN   Because of that jealousy – you hanged him?

LLYWELYN   Jealousy, yes, perhaps.
But you gave him the gallows.

SIWAN   Me? ... Me?

LLYWELYN   You thought it wise, in your contempt for me,
To try to sway my mind with political persuasion.
You thought I'd trade my desecrated bed
For a castle gained, that I'd accept
That my wife had been soiled, just to keep a pact
And secure borders.
I answered contempt with contempt.
I hanged him to make your threats become real,

	To show the wife who sullied me
	That there was one thing for which
	I'd throw away my crown and kingdom.
SIWAN	Llywelyn – Llywelyn!
	For that base urge to punish me
	You've fallen headlong into a war ... You're now almost sixty,
	Surely you know by now that government
	Isn't a matter of chancing and daring on a whim.
LLYWELYN	Your contempt for me that night
	Undid half a century's careful strategy.
SIWAN	That was the opposite of my intention.
LLYWELYN	The unintentional is the key to how history happens.
	That night your clenched mind opened and handed me
	A key to unlock mayhem.
SIWAN	You credit me with too much significance Llywelyn.
	We talked at cross purposes.
	You looked for an excuse.
	There were no keys passing from hand to hand.
	Not one single person on this earth
	Properly understands another.
	A husband embraces a wife.
	The wife responds with a kiss.
	Two planets, tied into their separate orbits.
	They'll never merge,
	They'll never share a common sphere.
LLYWELYN	That's what marriage is. Having the ties
	Without the common knowing.
	Drifting into it, uninformed, untutored –
	A grown man and a child are in the same trap.
	Each a victim of what's forced upon him, by chance.
	Lost in intricate games
	Where he had no say in drawing up the rules.
SIWAN	But war? That's by design, not chance.

LLYWELYN	And that depends on you. Will you come back to my table and my bed?
SIWAN	What does that have to do with war?
LLYWELYN	The war's inevitable now. You may still choose what you do with me.
SIWAN	I'm a prisoner. Your sentence separated us. Why not command me to come back to you.
LLYWELYN	You must come back of your own accord.
SIWAN	If I refuse?
LLYWELYN	Then – I'll go to war. And lead the fighting myself.
SIWAN	And not return? That threat's unworthy.
LLYWELYN	You, a princess and a king's daughter, You're well versed in threats and ultimata. They're part of our lives daily.
SIWAN	I can't come back to your bed Without your forgiveness.
LLYWELYN	You know that's been offered.
SIWAN	On your conditions. I won't grovel for Your forgiveness. I won't accept it either From a self obsessed hypocrite, I've listened to what you've told me. You say I've desecrated the royal bed. I also sent my lover to the gallows. I caused the South to fall to Hubert. I jeopardised Dafydd's kingdom and inheritance, I unstitched your sanity, wrecked your ordered world But you? You – are a martyr to a bad marriage. And now before you go to battle, you'll allow me Back into your bed. The royal bed. You'll devastate me with your gracious forgiving. You with the setting sun on your armour and helmet

As you ride to your worthy death.
When your body's brought back from battle
Should I commission a portrait from the court painter as a
    tribute
To the Man Who Was God?

The two laugh.

LLYWELYN   I'm not worthy of you Siwan.

SIWAN   Every married woman is told that
                    At one time or other. That's when their husbands
                    Are at their most dangerous.

LLYWELYN   Can you forgive me Siwan?

SIWAN   Llywelyn the Great asking forgiveness from a harlot?

LLYWELYN   That night, that twelvemonth back,
                    My love flamed into hate. Malice.
                    That night, I'll tell you, –

SIWAN   No. Don't tell me the truth.
                    This isn't a confessional. I'm no priest.
                    I'm a defeated woman who wants to win one more skirmish.

The two laugh again.

LLYWELYN   Will you forgive me Siwan?

SIWAN   For what? Calling me a whore?
                    The name sat on me easily enough.

LLYWELYN   The hanging. That fit of fury.
                    For relishing your anguish.

SIWAN   The residue of all this is your pitiful state.
                    Gwilym was hanged. He leapt to his death
                    Shouting my name. Our love was unbowed
                    In those last glorious seconds of defiance.
                    I'll remember him like that. We were spared
                    Any long disillusion, the cooling of passion,
                    Boredom becalming the flesh, and lies

Cheapening our talking. But you –
If you do forgive me
You'll have to live with the ashes of your old self.
With the nightmare of that night
When all love died within me. Sleeping with me
In that royal bed will be like
Lying in a grave, still alive. Can you, Llywelyn,
Put up with that? Can you not hate me?

LLYWELYN   Will you come back to me Siwan?

SIWAN   Between us in that bed
                Will be the stench of your trust's defiling.

LLYWELYN   If you return, between us in that bed
                Will be your lover's corpse swinging from a rope.

SIWAN   What shall we do with them Llywelyn?

LLYWELYN   Reach out our arms over them, and touch.
                Take them to us, between us, in penance.
                Purgatory's fires can mould a marriage's redemption.
                I'm the fire that blistered you, almost killed you,
                Tried to burn you to a cinder, you and the memory
                Of that boy who leapt to his death
                Still proclaiming his love for you.
                We've scorched each other. But not quite destroyed.
                Come back to me Siwan.

SIWAN   The habits of a quarter of a century bid me back.

LLYWELYN   Your son's whole future bids you back.

SIWAN   The daft ploys of an old man bent on a new war
                Bid me back.

LLYWELYN   Despite my age I might win that war
                And win you back.

SIWAN   Llywelyn, I wish you success,
                I wish you wellbeing ...

LLYWELYN   That's enough. You're as good as back already.

SIWAN	Will you take me back like that,
	With nothing but my goodwill?
LLYWELYN	Goodwill is love. Siwan, my wife,
	I'll come out of my chambers, ready for battle,
	I'll be eager and lusty. I'll smile a goodbye
	For you. I'll be fighting this war for you.
SIWAN	One word Llywelyn.
	I'll cheer your victory when it comes.
	I can see Hubert de Burgh's downfall.
	I can see the securing of Dafydd's great inheritance
	But after that, my days won't be many.
LLYWELYN	You'll live a long time after me.
SIWAN	No. I won't. Life still surges strongly in you.
	And your urge to succeed still drives you.
	I've lost that. Grant me one wish.
LLYWELYN	What's that?
SIWAN	My last testament. From the window of my prison loft
	Beyond the green where he was hanged,
	Over the Menai's waters I could see Dindaethwy
	And the rooks rising and settling in those woods
	By Saint Catrin's resting place.
	Seeing their freedom to glide and swoop, to nest
	And mate and squabble, high above men's to-ing and fro-ing
	Gladdened my heart, made me envious.
	When I die, take my body over the Menai
	Lay me to rest there and give the land
	To the Franciscan brothers to build a church.
LLYWELYN	The grey friars. Why Franciscans?
SIWAN	I owe a debt to the saint of the rope.
	He liked to chance his luck. To dice with death.
LLYWELYN	Your wish conceals some coded meaning.
	I thought you'd be buried with me in Aberconwy.

SIWAN	You referred to the marriage vows.
	They tie me to you until death. I abide by them.
	But the grave severs all such ties. Frees us all.
	I want my bones to crumble to dust
	With no one else beside me.

LLYWELYN   Alright, my heart. I'll do everything
            In accordance with your wishes Siwan.
            (*He calls*) Are you there Alis?

Alis enters.

ALIS   My lord?

LLYWELYN   Where's the royal crown of the Princess of Gwynedd?

Alis opens the chest.

ALIS   Here in ma dame's chest.

LLYWELYN   Bring it to me.
            This maid complains about you Siwan.

ALIS   Ma dame I do not. I never complain.

LLYWELYN   You haven't struck her for a year she says.
            She seems to miss the sting of your palm.

ALIS   Sir, my Lord, for shame on you.

LLYWELYN   And so, I'll take it upon myself to discipline her.
            If I return from the war victorious
            I'll give you away as a wife to the bravest lad
            In my retinue. And you'll thank me for that.
            The crown. My Princess, I crown you anew
            And give you half of Gwynedd's lands.
            I give you my right hand. I kiss your hand.
            We'll go to the great hall. We'll banquet.
            This afternoon I'll summon the councillors to Court
            And lay before them Gwynedd's new strategy for war.

END